For Eleanor & Walt

Barry

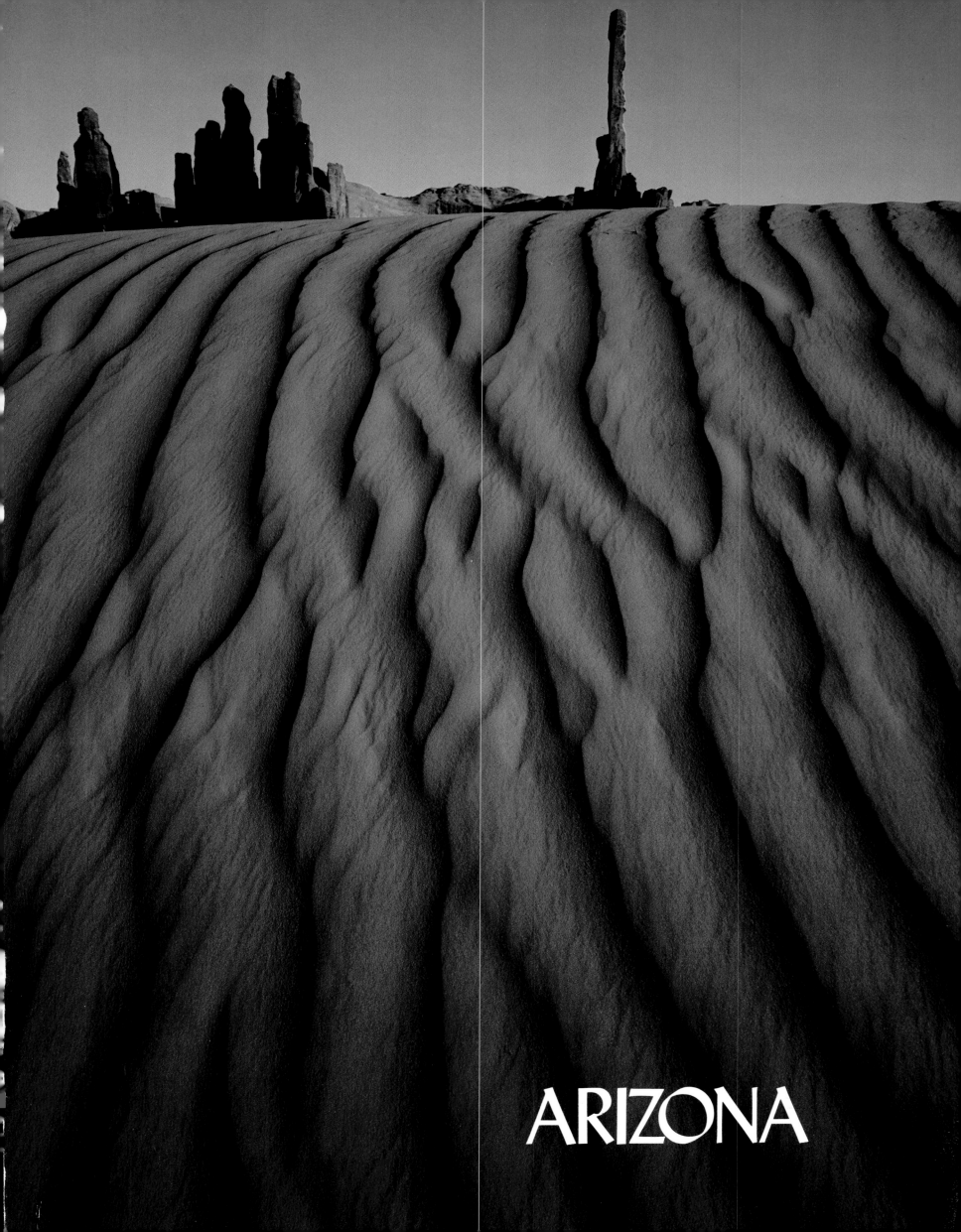

ARIZONA

Photography by DAVID MUENCH

ARIZONA

Text by BARRY GOLDWATER

RAND McNALLY & COMPANY
CHICAGO · NEW YORK · SAN FRANCISCO

Map of ARIZONA

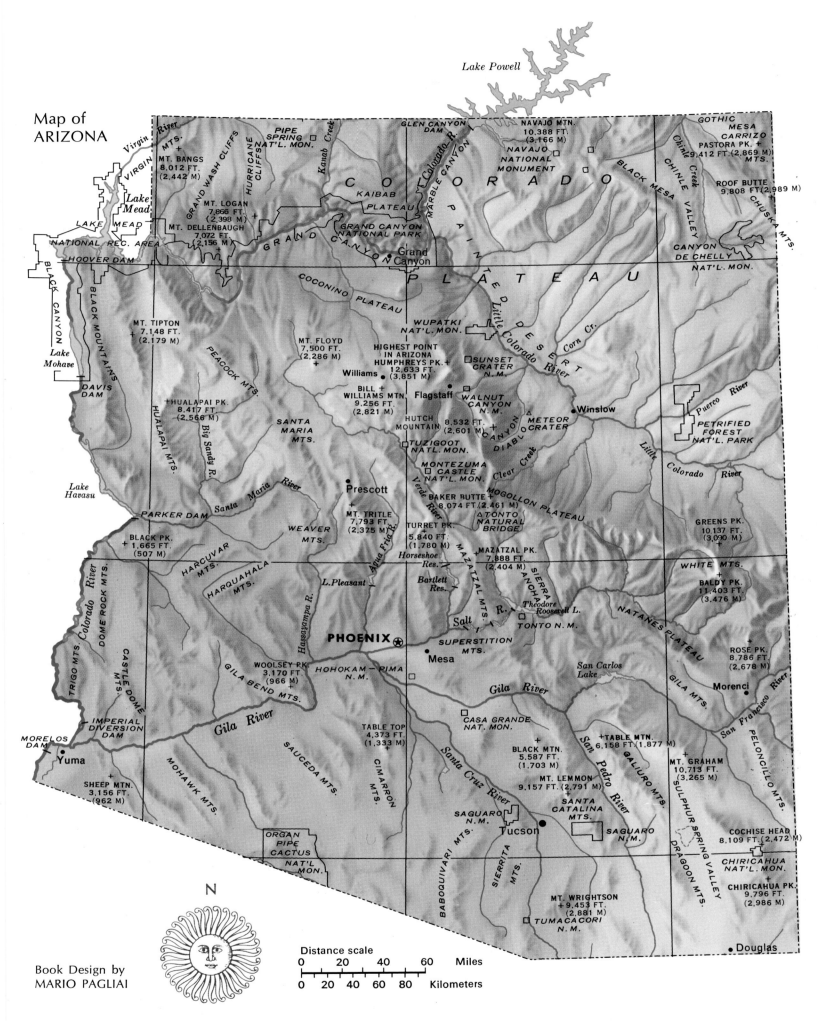

Lake Powell

N

Book Design by
MARIO PAGLIAI

Distance scale

| 0 | 20 | 40 | 60 | Miles |

| 0 | 20 | 40 | 60 | 80 | Kilometers |

Page one– ARTWORK OF EROSION, MONUMENT VALLEY NAVAJO TRIBAL PARK
Overleaf– SANDSTONE EYE, MONUMENT VALLEY

Library of Congress Cataloging in Publication Data

Goldwater, Barry Morris 1909–
  ARIZONA

  1. Arizona—Description and travel—1951–
I. Muench, David.   II. Title
F815.G64   979.1   78-7098
ISBN 0-528-81074-X

MEXICAN POPPIES, DOS CABEZAS MOUNTAINS

Contents

Prologue

HAVING BEEN BORN IN THE TERRITORY OF ARIZONA AND HAVING LIVED IN THE STATE ALL MY LIFE, I FEEL WELL QUALIFIED TO SERVE AS A SPOKESMAN FOR ARIZONA, TO PRAISE ITS SPLENDORS, TO CELEBRATE the spirit of its people. My family's roots reach far back into Arizona's past, and both sides of my family embody the pioneer spirit that made possible the settlement and growth of the state.

My father's father, Michael Goldwater, was impelled not only by the enterprising spirit that drove people west to make new lives for themselves on the frontier, but also by the yearning for religious freedom and a democratic way of life that led so many Europeans to leave the world of their fathers and cast their lot with the New World. "Big Mike" and his brother Joseph left their native Poland and, after brief stays in Germany and England, came to the United States in 1852. Once in this country, they became part of the great wave of emigrants who were lured to the California goldfields. In England they had worked as capmakers, and they started out in a humble way in America too, selling goods to men at the mining camps. My grandfather decided to move on once more, to what would become Arizona Territory, and later my great-uncle joined him. In Arizona the two brothers pulled themselves up by their bootstraps, as the saying goes, progressing from peddling to merchandising on a much larger scale. They opened a mercantile store in Prescott in 1872, and as it grew it branched out into other cities. My father, Baron Goldwater, carried on the family's flair for merchandising.

Goldwaters were involved in the early political life of Arizona as well as in its early commercial life. Both my grandfather and my uncle Morris served as mayor of Prescott, my grandfather briefly and my uncle for many years. Morris was chairman of the Central Territorial Committee, vice-president of the state Constitutional Convention in 1910, and later served as a state senator.

My mother, Josephine Williams Goldwater, was the daughter of parents who had traveled from Illinois to Nebraska in a covered wagon. Born in Nebraska, she carried the pioneering spirit in her very blood. She came to Arizona to recover from tuberculosis, and the climate here completely restored her health. She brought along with her her own nursing background, having earned an R.N. degree in Chicago, and I believe she was Arizona's first registered nurse. It was my mother who gave me my wanderlust and my love of the out-of-doors. We used to travel around the state in every conveyance known to man, and she taught my brother, sister, and me how to shoot, fish, camp out, and be strong. Above all, she imparted to me her great affection and respect for this state.

As for myself, I carry on the heritage of love for Arizona that was transmitted to me by my father and my mother. I was born in Phoenix on January 1, 1909, when Arizona was still a territory, so I grew up along with the state. I have followed my uncle's example in choosing to serve Arizona in a political capacity, entering politics in 1949, when I was elected to the City Council of Phoenix. In 1952 I began my career in the U.S. Senate.

Before going further, I would like to acknowledge the help I received on this book from the following people: my secretary Judy Eisenhower, who typed the rough drafts from my notes and comments; Dot Roberson, who worked through several versions of the manuscript; and Earl Eisenhower, who helped me verify the contents.

5

6

Introduction

WHEN I WAS ASKED TO WRITE THE NARRATIVE FOR A PHOTOGRAPHIC BOOK ON ARIZONA, I REALIZED THAT I WAS BEING OFFERED AN OPPORTUNITY TO EXPRESS MYSELF ABOUT THE TERRITORY IN which I was born and the state in which I was reared—the state I grew to love so much.

Someone once remarked that "beauty is in the eye of the beholder," and there is no horizon to my vision of Arizona's beauty. But when I saw David Muench's remarkable photographs, it became apparent that I would have a very difficult time writing a narrative that would match them in conveying the variety of the landscape and the beauty of my state. To tell the reader of this book something about the geography and history of Arizona, to describe the beauty that Muench's photographs have captured so gloriously, was to be a real challenge for a man who has spent a good part of his life arguing political matters.

My feelings about Arizona are deeper and broader than the Grand Canyon. Mingled with all of it is love: love of people, love of the land, love of country. With that in mind, please let me escort you on an armchair journey through the state that I have known so intimately all of my life. But before we start, I would like to give you a better understanding of the physical characteristics and the historical background of the Grand Canyon State.

With an area of almost 114,000 square miles, Arizona is the sixth largest of the fifty states. The federal government owns or controls approximately 70 percent of the land, including the Indian reservations, which occupy about one-fourth of the state. Though only some 15 percent of the land is in private hands—the rest is state-controlled—this adds up to the areas of Massachusetts, Connecticut, Delaware, and Rhode Island combined. The northern and northeastern section of the state is part of the Colorado Plateau, a region of deep canyons, broad mesas, desert, sandstone buttes, and high peaks. South of the plateau is mountain country, an irregular belt of ranges extending to the extreme southeast. Almost dividing the state in half in the eastern portion of this area is the Mogollon Rim, a rugged escarpment rising abruptly on the southern edge of the Mogollon Plateau. The southwest is a region of desert plains, the terrain broken up by small, barren mountains. In elevation, the land surface ranges from about 100 feet above sea level in the southwestern corner of the state to more than 12,000 feet in the mountains north of Flagstaff.

Arizona's climate varies widely, for the seasons depend not only upon the time of the year, but also upon the altitude of a particular area. Daytime summer temperatures in the southwest may soar to 120 degrees, but the nights are generally very comfortable because the humidity is extremely low. In the north-central desert areas, 5,000 to 8,000 feet above sea level, it is hot in the daytime—up to 95 degrees—and very cool when the sun goes down, while in the high mountain country south of here temperatures may be in the 60s and 70s during the day and a blanket or two will be needed at night. In the winter months it is possible to swim in the valleys of the southwestern desert or ski near Flagstaff or in the White Mountains in the east-central part of the state, where below-zero temperatures—minus 33 degrees in several places—have been recorded. As for spring and fall, again it depends upon the area. I recall very vividly that when my wife and I were first married, tears would come to her eyes each fall because the leaves on the trees didn't change color. Around Phoenix the leaves are a perpetual green. In the high country, at the same time of year, the aspen, oak, and maple leaves are changing into the most beautiful shades of gold and red and orange found anywhere on this earth. Fall in the northeastern part of the state might just as well be summer.

From the standpoint of precipitation, Arizona is a dry state. (*The flood-producing rainfall coupled with the exceptionally heavy snowfall early in 1978 was unusual.*) Only about 2 percent of the state is in harvested cropland, but 97 percent of this must be irrigated. On the average, the precipitation ranges from just a little over two inches a year near Yuma to less than forty inches in the White Mountains. In a typical year, the drier areas may go for months without rainfall. So scarce is water in Arizona that there are only about 120 square miles of natural lakes and just one river, the Colorado, with an appreciable flow of water. Dams built on the Salt, Verde, Agua Fria, and

Colorado rivers have created many man-made lakes. (On Fridays, out-of-state visitors who think of Arizona as one vast desert are surprised to find the roads leading to these lakes jammed bumper to bumper with cars trailing boats, the state's per-capita registration of which totals about 80,000.) Snowfall in the high mountains will often reach depths of almost ten feet, and the runoff from the melting snow provides most of the state's water supply. Unfortunately, there has never been enough precipitation to satisfy the everyday needs of a rapidly expanding population—almost doubled since 1960—so the people have come to depend, to a large degree, upon underground water. Many places in the state, particularly in the desert areas, are pumping water from wells faster than it is being replenished, and as a result the underground water table is being depleted. The only remedy outside of extreme conservation measures is to bring water from the Colorado River to the heavily populated valleys of south-central Arizona, and it was for this purpose that the Central Arizona Project was begun.

Despite the meager precipitation, Arizona's plant life is among the most varied in the United States, ranging from subtropical species to colorful flowers blooming in the snows of the mountain peaks. Grasses of many kinds provide excellent forage for livestock. About one-fourth of the state is forested, and most of the timbered areas are set aside in national preserves. Across the Mogollon Plateau stretches the largest stand of ponderosa pine in the United States. Representative of the numerous desert plants are the night-blooming cereus, Mexican poppy, Joshua tree, century plant, paloverde, and more than 100 varieties of cactus, including the giant saguaro and the hedgehog, barrel, prickly pear, and beavertail cacti with their showy blossoms.

Wildlife too is abundant and varied in the state. Deer, antelope, desert bighorn sheep, mountain lion, coyote, gray fox, elk, peccary, and black bear are some of the animals found here. Creatures typical of a desert environment are the Gila monster and other lizards, scorpion, tarantula, rattlesnake, and desert shrew. The many bird species include cactus wren, roadrunner, quail, wild turkey, mourning dove, and white-tailed dove. There are trout in the mountain streams and bass in the lakes.

Thus, contrary to the all-too-common conception of its being a desert, Arizona is instead a land of great contrasts, endowed with a diversity of physical features and climate.

As I sit in the study of my home on top of a hill some twelve miles from downtown Phoenix and look at the broad landscape of the city's buildings backed by the beautiful mountains called South Mountain and the Sierra Estrella to the south, I can't help but feel a great sense of pride in having lived with most of the development of this state. It hasn't been by accident that Arizona has become one of the leaders among the states. Plentiful and rich natural resources and the fine weather have helped, of course, but chiefly it has been its people—those who came first, those who were born here, the newcomers—who have made Arizona what it is today.

When Spanish explorers and missionaries entered what is now Arizona, they found many Indian tribes living there. Among these were the Hopi, Papago, and Pima, the descendants of tribes whose cultures died away long ago. The Hohokam, who constructed the finest irrigation system in prehistoric North America, were probably the forefathers of the Papago and Pima. Relatively new to the area were the Navajo and their kinsmen, the Apache, who splintered into several tribal groups. Wandering hunters, the Navajo settled in Arizona around the time of the arrival of the Spanish, as did the warlike Apache, probably the most nomadic of the Indian tribes.

In contrast to what is known about the Indians, who kept their history alive only by word of mouth, passing it down from one generation to another, considerable information is available about those who came after them. The earliest Spanish explorers had to report to their superiors in Mexico, so much of what they discovered has been recorded. In one instance, however, the authorities heard only what they wanted to believe, and in another they were told what they wanted to hear.

It was in 1539 that the first non-Indian, Fray Marcos de Niza, entered present-day Arizona territory. The Franciscan friar, who had been with Pizarro during the conquest of Peru, had come from Mexico City, and his mission was to verify Cabeza de Vaca's story about the fabled Seven Cities of Cíbola. Late in 1528 or early in 1529, Cabeza de Vaca, two other Spaniards, and a Moorish slave named Estevan had survived a shipwreck off the east coast of Texas. In what must surely be ranked as one of the greatest adventures of all time, the men worked their way across Texas, then south to Mexico, repeatedly being attacked and captured by Indians. Almost eight years and 5,000 miles later, they ended up in Mexico City. There the viceroy, Don Antonio de Mendoza, heard Cabeza de Vaca's descriptions of the long-lost Seven Cities of Cíbola, which lay to the north, cities whose streets were paved with silver, gold, and turquoise and whose houses were similarly adorned. Though he had also been told that the information had come from the Indians—and in sign language—the viceroy dispatched Fray Marcos, with Estevan the Moor as a guide, to confirm the story. The party started north and in the summer of 1539 entered what is now Arizona. Estevan, sent ahead as an advance guard, crossed the Gila River and continued in a northeasterly direction until he reached the land of the Zuñi Indians in present-day New Mexico. Here Estevan reportedly found one of the Seven Cities, and here he was killed by the Zuñi, possibly because of his unseemly attentions to their women. Fray Marcos, who probably never ventured beyond southern Arizona and relied on the flamboyant Estevan to keep him posted, returned to Mexico City. Unwilling to admit failure, he told fanciful stories about what he had discovered to the north. His report led to the organization of a large expedition under the command of Francisco Vásquez de Coronado to find and exploit the treasures of Cíbola. Guided by Fray Marcos, the expedition departed in 1540. Traveling the same general route Estevan had followed, Coronado discovered that the Seven Cities were nothing more than a group of Zuñi pueblos. After defeating the Zuñi, Coronado sent his lieutenants on far-ranging exploring missions. The various detachments encountered Hopi, Pima, Papago, and many lesser Indian tribes, providing the first written accounts of these people. Led by some of the Hopi, members of the expedition became the first non-Indians to see the Grand Canyon.

The Arizona region was to remain under Spanish control for almost 300 years, governed as part of the New Mexico province. During much of this time the search for precious metals continued as did efforts to explore and colonize the area and to conquer and Christianize the Indians. Intermittent attempts to convert the Hopi led to the Pueblo Revolt of 1680, after which the tribe sought security by moving to the top of the mesas where they are today. The most famous of the missionaries, Father Eusebio Francisco Kino, a Jesuit from Italy, was also a noted explorer. Much of what is known of southern Arizona's early history comes from the detailed accounts of his expeditions and the maps of the area—the first accurate ones drawn—he left behind. San Xavier del Bac (1700) was among some twenty-five missions he founded. (In the U.S. Capitol in Washington, D.C., is a statue of Father Kino, placed there in 1965 by the Arizona legislature.)

As a direct result of the Pima uprising of 1751, during which many missions were destroyed, including San Xavier (rebuilt later), a presidio—and the first white settlement in Arizona—was established at Tubac the following year. In 1776 the garrison was moved to a new presidio at Tucson, strategically located to fight off the Apache, who

BRISTLECONE ROOTS AGAINST HUMPHREYS PEAK

nevertheless gradually spread out over most of the Arizona region.

By the time Mexico won its independence from Spain, in 1821, and with it control of Arizona, the mission era had virtually ended. White immigrants, mostly from the Southern states, now began to settle in the area. Mexicans too moved in. When the United States went to war with Mexico in 1846, several American military expeditions crossed through Arizona but there were no battles in the area. The Mormon Battalion captured Tucson without a fight, for the garrison had abandoned the fort. With the signing of the Treaty of Guadalupe Hidalgo that ended the war in 1848, the land north of the Gila River was ceded to the United States, which proclaimed it a part of New Mexico Territory two years later. The area south of the Gila in both present-day Arizona and New Mexico was acquired from Mexico through the Gadsden Purchase of 1854.

Following the discovery of gold, silver, and copper in Arizona in the 1850s, many settlements were established, each new community encroaching on tribal lands and thus leading to increased hostilities between Indians and whites. The authorities responsible for handling these and other major problems were in far-off Santa Fe, more than 500 miles by stage from Tucson, the largest city in the Gadsden strip.

In 1860, after repeated petitions for creation of a separate territory comprising land in the Gadsden strip failed to pass in the U.S. Congress, a provisional government was formed and a Territory of Arizona proclaimed in Tucson. Most of the settlers had come from the Southern states, and just before the Civil War broke out, the provisional government voted to secede from the Union. When the war started, Federal troops in the area were removed, leaving the settlements and trade routes defenseless against Indian attack. Welcomed jubilantly, a confederate force commanded by Lieutenant Colonel John R. Baylor marched in from Texas in July 1861. Baylor took possession of the "Territory of Arizona" in the name of the Confederacy, a proclamation formalized by Jefferson Davis the following February. Two short months later, however, Federal troops were in control of the whole area. The only "battle" between the Union and Confederate forces in Arizona occurred in April of 1862 when scouting parties of both sides surprised each other at Picacho Pass. The net result of this "battle" was five dead and two Confederates captured. Thereafter, the Confederates retreated back across New Mexico.

Congress finally signed the bill creating Arizona Territory in February 1863. Except for a section of land in the northwest that was turned over to Nevada in 1866, the boundaries were the same as the state's are today. John A. Gurley of Ohio, appointed the first territorial governor, died before he could leave the East, and John N. Goodwin of Maine succeeded him. Goodwin and the other government officials reached Arizona on December 27, 1863, and took the oath of office at Navajo Springs two days later. Fort Whipple served as the temporary capital until a new site was selected twenty miles away, and here, where the Governor's Mansion was built in 1864, the town of Prescott was laid out. (The capital was

9

moved to Tucson in 1867, then back to Prescott in 1877, and finally to Phoenix in 1889.) In the census of the territory taken the same year, the white population totaled 4,573, and I'm very proud that my grandfather's name was among those on that first list. So was my great-uncle Joseph's. After the Civil War, most of Arizona was still the Indian's domain, and though new army posts were established, they were too widely scattered to protect the vast territory, especially from marauding Apache tribes who raided almost at will not only the white settlements but the camps of other Indian tribes as well. The whites believed that the land was as much theirs as the Indians', having won it from Mexico. They also thought that the Indians should be "civilized," and what better way than by settling the various tribes on their own reservations, where they would live in peace and learn the white man's ways. The methods used to accomplish this were sometimes ruthless, as was the case with the Navajo in 1864–1868. The Papago, Pima, Maricopa, and even friendly Apache tribes aided a succession of commanders in subjugating most of the hostile Apache by 1872 and the Yavapai by 1873. Finally, with the capture in 1886 of Geronimo and his Apache band, who had fled the reservation, the Indian wars in Arizona came to an end.

As the danger from Indian raids gradually lessened, new immigrants were drawn to Arizona. Mormons from Utah founded many communities, the first group of pioneers to settle on the farmlands. Towns sprang up following new gold strikes, and when these deposits played out, silver became the attraction. The rich veins of silver discovered at Tombstone brought in such a horde of prospectors, then merchants to supply the mining district, that soon the town was the largest in Arizona, boasting a population of some 10,000. The surrounding area also boomed, spurring the completion of a transcontinental railroad across the Southwest in 1882, the western extension reaching Tucson in 1880. Tombstone's glory days lasted less than a decade, but its wild West frontier character has become legendary. Miners fanning out from Tombstone in search of new strikes found large copper deposits at Bisbee and elsewhere. These, however, were considered to be practically worthless until the electrical revolution and the resultant demand for copper wiring. Today Arizona produces over 50 percent of the nation's supply of the mineral, which has provided more income for the state than the gold and silver mines combined.

Large-scale cattle and sheep ranching began with the coming of the railroads. The inevitable conflicts between cattlemen and sheepmen over the use of grazing land lasted until both groups were confronted with competition from a third group—the homesteaders, whose settlements were to end the era of the unfenced range. The Homestead Act of 1862 had allotted land to anyone willing to improve it, but fear of Indian raids had discouraged many pioneers from taking advantage of the offer. A second federal act stipulated that some of the free acreage be planted in trees. To encourage settlement in the arid sections of the state, the Desert Land Act of 1877 gave homesteaders title to 640 acres, but only if they would irrigate the land. Prior to passage of this last act, some farming had already started in the Salt River Valley,

where water for irrigation was available. A man by the name of Jack Swilling, who was visiting the area in 1867, noticed what appeared to be ruins of ancient canals near the river. Realizing their purpose, he organized a canal company to take advantage of the ditches to bring water to the land. Shortly thereafter a small community sprang up as families settled along both banks of the Salt, to begin irrigation farming. This little community would enjoy a phenomenal growth, for it was the start of the city of Phoenix, destined to become the center of Arizona's largest metropolitan area.

During the following decades Mormon farmers established settlements in the Salt and Gila valleys and in the east-central part of the state. By now the original ditches were no longer adequate for irrigation purposes, and other canal companies were founded to do the job. But as the population centers grew so did the demand for water and for solutions to the cycles of flooding and drought that plagued the valley settlements. The answer was the construction of large dams, and with federal funds the first of Arizona's major reclamation projects, the Theodore Roosevelt Dam on the Salt River, was built. The president himself dedicated the dam in 1911.

The territory now had a sound economic base and an excellent transportation network, with two transcontinental railroads serving the growing cities, and was well on the way toward solving its water problem. It was time to concentrate on achieving statehood.

As early as 1892 a bill in favor of Arizona statehood had passed in the U.S. House of Representatives but died in the Senate. One of the stumbling blocks in the years that followed was a proposal to combine the New Mexico and Arizona territories into a single state with the capital at Santa Fe. Congress later made this motion contingent on acceptance by the citizens of both territories, and in the election, held in 1906, Arizonans voted a resounding No.

In June 1910, Congress finally passed the enabling act that authorized Arizona to draft a state constitution. My uncle Morris, one of the delegates elected to the Constitutional Convention, was chosen its vice-president. The following year, after the people approved the document, Congress voted to admit Arizona to the Union, but President William Howard Taft vetoed the bill. For its day, the state's constitution was a liberal one. It was even called radical. Among its reform features were women's suffrage; direct election of U.S. senators, at a time when they were still being appointed; direct primaries; popular election of judges; and the initiative, referendum, and recall. It was the recall of judges that Taft objected to. Congress passed a new resolution deleting this clause, and on February 14, 1912, the president signed the proclamation making Arizona the forty-eighth state of the Union. (In the first state election, the recall clause was restored.)

Arizona has always been a progressive state. Its citizens had framed a constitution that in essence created a state government responsible to, and under the control of, the people. I'm proud to say that many of the provisions considered radical at the time have been adopted by other states.

10

ARIZONA

12

INDIAN COUNTRY

THE FIRST WHITE MEN TO TRAVERSE WHAT IS NOW CALLED ARIZONA WERE EN ROUTE TO PRESENT-DAY NEW MEXICO, WHERE THEY HOPED TO FIND THE FABLED WEALTH OF THE SEVEN CITIES OF CÍBOLA. THOUGH THE SEVEN CITIES proved to be humble Zuñi pueblos, the whites did find a wealth of Indian cultures in the Southwest, and Indians continue to play a major role in Arizona today. The largest concentration of Indian land in the state—the Navajo and Hopi reservations—is in the northeastern corner, the Four Corners area where Arizona touches Utah, Colorado, and New Mexico. These two reservations comprise the heart of what Arizonans call the Indian Country, covering the northern sections of Navajo and Apache counties and northeastern Coconino County. The fascination of this area is by no means limited to the Indian life it supports, for it is also known for its spectacular natural beauty.

The Navajo Indian Reservation is the largest in the United States, covering some 24,000 square miles. It is not confined to Arizona, but extends into New Mexico and Utah as well. The Navajo reservation is also the country's largest in terms of population, with nearly 150,000 Indians living on or near it, and more than half of them in Arizona. No one is certain what the name Navajo means. Some people associate it with the Spanish words for "fighting knife," but this cannot be backed up by research. The Navajo call themselves the Dineh, which is the tribal word for "people."

A good place to begin one's acquaintance with the Navajo's way of life is the town of Window Rock, capital of the Navajo nation. Located in the southeastern part of the Indian Country near the New Mexico border, the town was named for a large, natural hole in the sandstone cliff above it. Window Rock is the site of the Tribal Council Headquarters, which was begun in 1933 and completed in 1936. The Tribal Council was formed by consolidating five separate agencies that had served the Navajo up to that time. Every year in early September, the Indians gather in Window Rock from the far reaches of the reservation for the Navajo Nation Fair, which includes a rodeo, exhibits of handicrafts, and Navajo dances. This is a marvelous time to see the young and the old mixing their time-honored ways with those of the modern world.

If it is true that the pickup truck has revolutionized the modern-day cowboy, then it is doubly true of the Navajo. I can remember when, not too many years ago, these people all traveled by horseback or horse-drawn wagon. Because of this limitation, the outlying trading post was the center of the average Navajo's life. Today, however, with the advent of faster means of transportation, the Navajo's life-style is changing as they are reaching out into a world that was beyond their grasp just a few short years ago.

The present-day Navajo are leaving behind some of their traditional ways, but the inner core of their spiritual life remains intact. The Navajo religion is based on nature worship and spiritualism. Their medicine men perform pretty much the same functions as the clergymen in other faiths, but they do their spiritual healing by sprinkling sacred corn and making sand paintings. A medicine man works from sunrise until nightfall on the sand painting that will heal the ills of one of his patients. He does this with the distinct understanding on his part and on the part of his patient that, whatever the illness may be, once the patient has placed himself or herself upon the sand painting, the sickness will disappear. After the ritual is completed, the sand painting is completely destroyed.

The Navajo also have their "sings." These are gatherings of the Navajo community that, to a large extent, resemble the Christian ritual of going to church and singing hymns. A sing can involve a prayer of thanks, a prayer for well-being, or a combination of the two. When the word goes out to the community that one of these ceremonies is in the offing, the Navajo begin gathering from miles around. In earlier days, when I owned a trading post, I was privileged to be invited to some sings, and I found them to be delightful and moving experiences. The Navajo would arrive by horseback and horse-drawn wagon with enough necessities to last two or three days. The host—the Navajo who had called for the sing—supplied several sheep, corn bread, and other food to feed the multitude. The actual rituals were held at night around a huge bonfire fed with juniper and cedar logs. Since I was a white man, I was not allowed to participate in the ceremony, but I could be there as an observer. Rolled up in my sleeping bag, I savored the fragrant aroma of the

13

fire drifting across the plain. These sings have to be some of my most cherished memories.

For those who would like to catch a glimpse of the older way of the Navajo, I suggest a short trip to a place about thirty miles west of Window Rock. Here, at Ganado, is located the famous Hubbell Trading Post. Now a national historic site, it is still in operation just as it was some seventy or eighty years ago. The historic site also houses collections of paintings, Indian crafts, firearms, and books. Originally established in 1811, the post was bought by "Don Lorenzo" Hubbell in 1876. He promptly named the place Ganado after his friend Ganado Mucho, who was the last peace chief of the Navajo. Don Lorenzo thought so much of his friend that Ganado Mucho was buried in the Hubbells' hilltop cemetery, overlooking the trading post. Not only was Don Lorenzo a great friend of the Navajo, but he was also largely responsible for reviving the rug-weaving tradition in the tribe and raising the quality of the work to the standard of a fine art. Today, a "Ganado Red" Navajo rug is one of the finest examples of native American craftsmanship.

The communities of Klagetoh and Wide Ruins, south of Ganado, are also places that afford insight into the traditional life-style of the Navajo. This is hill country, covered with bunchgrass and scrub cedar, and very often young Navajo girls can be seen tending the herds of sheep as they graze over the land.

A few miles north of Window Rock is Fort Defiance, which is now the center of the Tribal Health Service. Founded in September 1851, it was the first permanent American military post to be established in what is now Arizona. Its existence is testimony to the conflicts between Indians and whites that were common in the nineteenth century. Located at the mouth of Bonito Canyon, the post was built by Colonel Edwin V. Sumner and a contingent of soldiers from Santa Fe to serve as a military stronghold deep within the area claimed by the Navajo. Hence the name—the purpose of the fort was to *defy* the Navajo. Fort Defiance was almost continuously in action until Kit Carson subdued the Navajo in 1863–1864. With the treaty of 1868, it became the headquarters of the Navajo Indian Agency. Since that time all of the land and buildings have been given to the tribe.

The Navajo reservation is a fascinating place to visit not only for the lessons it teaches about the Navajo's way of life, but also for the splendor of its high desert terrain and for the traces that remain of ancient Indian civilizations. Amid the stark beauty of this desert is one of the most spectacular natural wonders in the world—Canyon de Chelly National Monument. (The name *de Chelly*, pronounced "da SHAY," is based on the Navajo words meaning "rock canyon," filtered through Spanish.) Covering more than 80,000 acres in the eastern part of the reservation, the monument actually includes several stream-cut canyons, the largest of which—thirty-five miles long—is Canyon del Muerto.

Canyon de Chelly was once the home of the prehistoric Anasazi people. (*Anasazi* is the Navajo word for "The Ancient Ones.") Two of the best-preserved pueblo dwellings, Antelope House and White House, are built into the red sandstone canyon walls far above the valley floor. Their protected position accounts for their good condition. Also to be seen are pictographs—in caves, on the canyon walls, and on the striking 800-foot-high Spider Rock. The Navajo tribe moved into Canyon de Chelly from northern New Mexico around 1700, four centuries after its abandonment by the Anasazi, and it was granted to them as part of their reservation under the peace treaty of 1868. The national monument was established in 1931, but some of the Navajo still regard it as their home. Today, visitors can see Navajo Indians living, farming, and grazing their sheep in the shadows of the ancient buildings of the Anasazi.

Northeast of Canyon de Chelly are the Chuska Mountains, which attain heights close to 9,000 feet. (Their name comes from the Navajo word for "white spruce" or "fir.") While they are not the tallest mountains and do not cover nearly as much area as some others do, they are certainly among the most beautiful in the state. Covered with pine, oak, aspen, and maple trees, these mountains have been the refuge of the Navajo for centuries. It was to the Chuskas that the Navajo medicine men would journey in search of the mystical powers they needed to help their people.

The southern and southwestern parts of the Navajo reservation are dominated by the Painted Desert. Almost without vegetation, this desert nevertheless has a beauty all its own. The entire area was, at one time or other, covered by water, which built up multicolored layers of sediments. The subsequent erosion has created colorful effects similar to what an energetic child might produce with a paintbrush and a box of tempera paints. The intensity of the brilliant hues changes with the variations in the light, heat, and dust particles in the air.

At the eastern edge of the Painted Desert, just south of the Navajo reservation, is another legacy from Arizona's geological past—the Petrified Forest, which became a national park in 1962. Some of the most magnificent stretches of the Painted Desert fall within the park's boundaries. Covering more than 94,000 acres, the park consists of six "forests" of brightly colored logs-turned-to-stone, their cells long since filled in with silica and other minerals. The Anasazi Indians placed a high value on petrified wood, using pieces of it as tools and weapons, and it has retained its appeal, but for a different reason. The splendor of the Petrified Forest attracts many visitors to this part of Arizona.

Some of the best-preserved Indian ruins in the United States can be found in the Painted Desert area. North of Flagstaff, just southwest of the Navajo reservation, is Wupatki National Monument, established in 1924. (*Wupatki* is the Hopi word for "tall house.") Here are some 800 ruins dating back to the Anasazi Indians of the twelfth century A.D. It is through places like this, where ancient dwellings have been preserved, that researchers can study and reconstruct the lives and environment of America's early settlers. The archaeologists who excavated the Wupatki ruins came upon a ball court, evidence of the importance of games in the Indians' lives. Other ruins excavated at Wupatki are an amphitheater and some pueblo-type dwellings, such as Wupatki Ruin and Citadel Ruin. They are well worth visiting.

The lives of the Indians who inhabited this area were touched by a natural phenomenon eighteen miles to the south—Sunset Crater, which became a national monument in 1930. The crater erupted in 1065, making it the youngest member of the San Francisco Peaks Volcanic Field. The eruption frightened the Indians in the vicinity and caused them to flee, but it also spread a blanket of volcanic ash over some 800 square miles, improving the quality of the soil. The now-fertile land drew several Indian groups to the area, including those who left the Wupatki ruins. The Indians flourished in the shadow of Sunset Crater until they were driven out by a drought that began in 1215.

In the northwestern part of Arizona's Indian Country are the unusual rock formations known as the Vermilion Cliffs and the Echo Cliffs. The Vermilion Cliffs extend for about twenty miles across the plateau west of the Colorado River, which forms the western boundary of the Navajo Indian Reservation. Reaching heights of more than 1,000 feet, they are colored in brilliant shades of red, orange, and green. The Echo Cliffs, on the east side of the Colorado River, are also known for their striking

GREGG ARCH, CHUSKA MOUNTAINS

colors. They got their name in 1869 from Major John Wesley Powell's party, a member of which shot his revolver into the stretch of river below them and produced a series of resonating echoes.

The northern stretch of the Indian Country falls within Monument Valley, which straddles the Utah-Arizona border from Lake Powell to the Four Corners area. There are many, many things to be seen in the valley, where a person can spend months traveling without doubling back and see something new every hour of the day. Monument Valley was named for the beautiful red sandstone formations that keep silent watch over its desert terrain. These eroded, wind-carved "monuments" were originally formed by the water that once covered the area. The sand and other debris in the water settled to the bottom, where the great pressure of the water above them hardened them into stone. As the water receded, it cut canyons by eroding the relatively soft sandstone. Also to be seen in the valley are ancient ruins and traditional Navajo hogans.

The Indian ruins in the northern part of Arizona's Indian Country are as remarkable as those in the southwestern part. I am referring to Navajo National Monument, established in 1909. Its 600 acres shelter some priceless traces of twelfth-century cliff-dwelling Indians—Inscription House Ruin, Keet Seel ("broken pottery" in Navajo), Betatakin ("ledge house"), and other, smaller ruins. Inscription House is closed to visitors and Keet Seel is difficult to get to, but Betatakin, one of the state's most spectacular cliff ruins, can easily be visited on foot. Keet Seel, with 160 rooms, is the largest cliff dwelling in Arizona. Only a limited number of visitors are allowed in Keet Seel and Betatakin per day, to minimize the damage done to these fragile structures.

While the Navajo are predominant in northeastern Arizona, they nevertheless share this area with the Hopi, whose name means "The Peaceful Ones." The Hopi Indian Reservation, which is completely surrounded by the Navajo, is located on the southern edge of Black Mesa. Some 6,900 Hopi live on or near the 650,172-acre reservation. There is also a Navajo-Hopi Joint Use Area, but plans are under way to make a permanent division of this land. The Hopi villages are situated atop three fingerlike extensions that are named First, Second, and Third Mesa. The Hopi chose the mesas—flat-topped mountains—for their dwellings because of the protection they afforded. It was relatively easy for the tribesmen to defend the path leading up to the cliff and hard for their enemies to climb it. Below the villages, in the sandy soil of the washes, are the farms of these Pueblo Indians.

On the Hopi reservation is the ancient village of Oraibi, believed to be one of the oldest continuously inhabited towns in the United States, with the Hopi and their ancestors having lived there since the twelfth century. Today, Old Oraibi is the last refuge of those Hopi who maintain a strict adherence to their ancient ways, while some of the newer towns such as Bacobi and Hotevilla have become noted for their annual kachina dances and snake dance. Walpi, a village perched atop First Mesa, is also noted for its dances.

The Hopi are an industrious people who have managed to maintain their heritage and living patterns much the way they were when the first Spanish explorers arrived. Their dry-farming techniques, for example, are probably little changed over hundreds of years.

Like the Navajo, the Hopi have remained faithful to the past in their religion. During the period between the winter and summer solstices the Hopi pay homage to their gods to ensure the growth of adequate crops, believing, for example, that if they perform the bean dance with proper respect, the seeds will germinate better. Their gods are related mostly to their everyday wants, so a ceremony held in the square of the pueblo is, in essence, a prayer to a particular god, or to several gods, for whatever will meet their needs of the moment. All the ceremonies are held at a traditional time.

An important aspect of the Hopi's religion is their belief in kachinas. The visitor to Arizona will hear the word *kachina* very often, and he will probably hear it first connected with dolls. To the Hopi, kachinas are supernatural beings—more than 200 in number—who have power over every aspect of their lives. The kachina dolls that a visitor will see in almost every Indian store and trading post in Arizona are not used directly for religious worship. They are carved by the father of the family to use for instructing the children. Familiarity with the dolls will enable the boy or girl to recognize the various kachinas when they are embodied by dancers performing in a ceremony in the pueblo. The children are initiated into the kachina cult at an early age, and they spend their entire lives devoted to the religion passed on to them by the tribal fathers.

My personal interest in kachina dolls goes back to the first time I visited the Hopi reservation. I was taken there by an old friend, John Rinker Kibbey, when I was seven years old. After World War II and just before he passed away, I bought his large collection of the dolls to add to mine, and I continued to add to it over the years. In 1964 I presented the collection to the Heard Museum of Anthropology and Primitive Arts in Phoenix, where it can be viewed today along with the beautiful collection that came from the Fred Harvey family.

The Hopi's artistic representations of kachinas include masks as well as dolls. The Hopi chiefs occasionally travel through the deserts and forest to the top of the San Francisco Peaks, where they sit and watch their different gods walking through the forest. They then return to their villages and make masks to depict what they saw in the forest. These masks often reflect varying interpretations of what a kachina looks like, for each chief sees the god through his own eyes. The variations are not great, however, and there is unanimous agreement regarding the appearance of the twelve highest deities. The Hopi believe that when a man puts on one of these masks and his body is also properly adorned, he himself will acquire godlike powers.

The kachina is a fascinating part of Arizona culture, and the Hopi's adherence to the kachina faith is a beautiful example to all persons who have strong feelings about their own religions.

16

21

22

Left– WHITE HOUSE, CANYON DE CHELLY NATIONAL MONUMENT
Below– ROCK FORMATIONS AND JUNIPER *and Overleaf–* SANDSTONE PILLARS
IN MONUMENT VALLEY NAVAJO TRIBAL PARK

Overleaf– YEBECHAI ROCK FORMATIONS, MONUMENT VALLEY NAVAJO TRIBAL PARK
Above– SANDSTONE MONOLITHS *and Right*– LINES OF TIME IN MONUMENT VALLEY

32

Left– BETATAKIN and Below– KEET SEEL IN NAVAJO NATIONAL MONUMENT
Overleaf– EVENING MOOD, CHUSKA MOUNTAINS

Above– VERMILION CLIFFS
Right– DESERT FLOOR BELOW ECHO CLIFFS

40

Above– WHITE MESA ARCH *and Right–* WHITE MESA AND
A NAVAJO HOGAN IN NAVAJO INDIAN RESERVATION

Above– VOLCANIC TABLEAU, SUNSET CRATER NATIONAL MONUMENT
Below– PETROGLYPH, TSEGI CANYON
Right– WUKOKI RUIN, WUPATKI NATIONAL MONUMENT

CANYON COUNTRY

WHILE NORTHEASTERN ARIZONA IS DOMINATED BY THE NAVAJO AND HOPI INDIAN RESERVATIONS, WHICH WERE ESTABLISHED BY GOVERNMENTAL ACTS, NORTHWESTERN ARIZONA IS DOMINATED by monumental works of nature—by canyons, especially the Grand Canyon, and by the river whose relentlessly driving force etched the canyons into the land. The Colorado River, creator of the Grand Canyon, enters Arizona from Utah at the northwestern corner of the Navajo reservation, twists its way south and west as far as Black Canyon, then turns south to form most of Arizona's western boundary. After leaving Arizona it cuts through part of Mexico on its way to the Gulf of California.

The Colorado is the largest river in Arizona, and it is a vital source of water for the state. A Supreme Court ruling in 1963 allotted Arizona a yearly quota of 2,800,000 acre-feet of water from the river. To bring the Colorado's water to Phoenix and Tucson, which are now tapping and depleting the water table, construction of the Central Arizona Project was begun.

For centuries the Colorado River has challenged and intrigued the human imagination. The first white man known to have seen the Colorado was a Spaniard named Francisco de Ulloa, who sailed up the Gulf of California in 1539. When he saw the gigantic tidal bore of the river and heard its terrifying noises, he turned around and sailed away. In 1540 a braver soul, Captain Hernando de Alarcón, overcame the terrors of the river's mouth and traveled up it "some eighty leagues," as far as the present site of Yuma, in an unsuccessful attempt to take supplies to the Coronado expedition. He gave the river its first Spanish name, *El Río de Buena Guía,* or "The River of Good Guidance."

Other names followed, reflecting the explorers' interests and their impressions of the river. Because the Indians who lived along the shores kept themselves warm by holding burning brands in their hands, Captain Melchior Díaz, traveling overland through northern Sonora to search for Alarcón, called the river *Río del Tizón* (Firebrand River). In 1604 Juan de Oñate came upon the Colorado at the mouth of what is now called the Bill Williams River. Oñate named it *Río Grande de Buena Esperanza* (The Great River of Good Hope). Father Eusebio Kino, who also observed Indians holding firebrands at the mouth of the river, called it *Río de los Martires* (River of the Martyrs). Kino's lieutenant gave it the name *Río del Norte* (River of the North), and this appears on many early maps.

The Indians, who had known the river long before the coming of the Spanish, gave it names that described its physical characteristics. The Cocomaricopa named it for its size, the Paiute for the depth of its canyons. The Pima and Yuma both gave it names meaning "red," because that is the color of the land it flows through. The present-day name of the river has the same meaning as theirs, though many people are unaware that *Colorado* comes from the Spanish words *color rojo,* or "red color."

Through the centuries the Colorado River has cut canyon after canyon in many types of rock. Its most spectacular creation, of course, is the Grand Canyon, which is the heart of Arizona's Canyon Country, but some of its smaller canyons fall within the state's boundaries as well. One of these—Glen Canyon—was cut into the rock at the point where the river enters Arizona from Utah. Today Glen Canyon lies beneath the water of man-made Lake Powell, which is part of the 1,236,880-acre Glen Canyon National Recreation Area. (Lake Powell was formed by building Glen Canyon Dam across the river.) The recreation area, which straddles the Arizona-Utah border, is a popular place for camping and hiking, as well as water sports.

Just downstream from the Glen Canyon National Recreation Area is Marble Canyon. Formerly a national monument, it was made part of Grand Canyon National Park in 1975. The fifty-mile stretch of the Colorado River that flows through Marble Canyon is known for its frequent rapids, and the canyon walls loom over the river, reaching heights of 3,000 feet.

The Grand Canyon is the Colorado River's masterpiece. It is my favorite place in the entire world, and I have often said that if I ever had a mistress, it would be the Grand Canyon.

All of the Grand Canyon falls within Arizona, in Coconino and Mohave counties. Exactly how it was formed has become a matter of contention among geologists, but their disputes cannot take away any of its magnificence. The Grand Canyon is truly one of the Seven Natural Wonders of the world. It has been protected as a national park since 1919, and the park was nearly doubled in size—to more than 1,200,000 acres—in 1975. Grand Canyon National Park stretches for over 150 miles, from the Glen Canyon National Recreation Area to Lake Mead.

The fascination of the Grand Canyon lies not only in its physical splendor and its geological mysteries, but also in the human drama it has encompassed. When I was a boy, anyone who suggested that people might have lived in the canyon at one time would be thought of as "poco loco," but a person making the same statement today has evidence to back him up. Archaeologists have found several hundred different sites in the Grand Canyon where people once lived, and some of the artifacts taken from the sites may date back as far as 4,000 years. The identity of these people—whether they were forerunners of present-day Indians or a long since withered branch of the family of man—remains nebulous. It is known, however, that from time immemorial the Hopi and their ancestors have made a yearly journey into the inner reaches of the canyon, their destination being a natural salt outcropping. Because of its deep religious significance, this journey of the Hopi's can be undertaken only by the spiritual leaders of their tribe.

García Lopez de Cárdenas, a member of the Coronado expedition of 1540, was the first white man to see the Grand Canyon. Coronado had sent him there to check out Indians' tales of a large river in the vicinity. But the canyon was not officially explored until the mid-1800s. A topographical engineer of the U.S. Army Corps of Engineers, Joseph C. Ives, ventured up the Colorado River in 1857–1858. Ives did not reach the main gorge of the Grand Canyon by boat, but he did reach it by land, and—ironically—he described it as an area that would never be worthy of anyone's attention. The first river journey through the Grand Canyon was made by the Powell expedition. Bent on exploring and charting this vast, unknown terrain, Major John Wesley Powell and nine other men set out from Green River, Wyoming, on May 24, 1869. They guided their four boats down the Green River into the Colorado, passing through canyons that white men had never seen before. The expedition was a real challenge to the bravery of these men, for they had heard rumors from Indians and trappers that the river plunged underground and cascaded in giant waterfalls. Powell not only accomplished his mission—five others in his party completed the incredibly difficult, more than three-month journey—but made the trip again two years later. Americans are indebted to the one-armed Civil War veteran for the names of many of the formations in and around the canyon, including Glen Canyon, Marble Canyon, and the Grand Canyon itself.

The canyon can be approached from the south by way of Flagstaff or Williams, or from the east on the road running from Cameron to the village of Grand Canyon, where the famous old (1905) El Tovar Hotel is located. The eastern road is probably more interesting. From Desert View on into the village, it provides a constant view of the canyon and a wealth of places where visitors can stop to take pictures. The eastern road continues along the South Rim for about eight miles past the El Tovar to Hermits Rest, which is a delightful spot to visit. This is the head of Hermit Canyon, and at one time the only trail down into the Grand Canyon started here.

The North Rim of the Grand Canyon is about twelve miles from here as the crow flies, but it is a 215-mile drive. From the North Rim a person can look down on the South Rim, which averages about 1,200 feet lower. The canyon can be approached from the north by way of Jacob Lake, one of the most beautiful drives in the world. It passes through some of the largest stands of ponderosa pine to be seen in Arizona, and there are side roads that lead to such outstanding lookouts as Cape Royal and Point Imperial, the highest point—8,801 feet—on the North Rim.

I first saw the Grand Canyon when I was about seven years old. Two years later I went down the trail to the river, and since that time I have probably walked down every available trail in the canyon. I've made three trips through the canyon by boat, the first one in 1940. These boat trips could never lose their tremendous thrill for me.

People often ask me to recommend the best way to see the Grand Canyon or the best time to see it, meaning not only time of day, but time of year. To tell the truth, it is absolutely breathtaking and beautiful at any time and in any season. But my favorite way to see the Grand Canyon is to rise before the sun even thinks of getting up, find a seat on the edge of the rim, and just sit and watch as the light of the dawning sun begins to illuminate the rock formations in the canyon, painting them from top to bottom. Then I can witness the same thing in reverse in the evening by going to another particularly beautiful point of the canyon to watch as the last rays of the setting sun work their magic. The colors change, the shapes change, and I get a glimpse of God's work that no other place can provide.

Wintertime gives the Grand Canyon a special aura. After a heavy snowfall, everything in the canyon seems to be different, for what was red the day before is now enveloped in a white mantle. The snow-covered canyon gleaming beneath the bright light of a full moon is one of the most beautiful sights I have ever seen, but the other seasons of the year produce splendors of their own.

There are many good trails for hikers, such as Bright Angel and Kaibab, and the Grand Canyon can also be tackled on muleback. The river trip through the canyon now attracts some 15,000 people a year, and there are helicopters that fly adventurous souls to remote parts of the park for unusual studies or for taking photographs. The Grand Canyon appeals to so many different interests that I doubt anyone could see it and not want to see it again. I visit the canyon every January along with a group of friends, and we have been doing this every year since World War II. And, while the group changes, the canyon never does.

Any discussion of the Grand Canyon would be incomplete if there were no mention of the Havasupai Indians, who live down in a branch of the canyon, their reservation half encircled by the national park. The

48

Havasupai, whose name means "People of the Blue-Green Water," moved to this area hundreds of years ago from central Arizona and adopted a way of life similar to that of the Pueblo Indians. They were one of the last Indian tribes to be exposed to the white man's culture. On the Havasupai reservation are several extremely beautiful waterfalls, all formed by Havasu Creek. These are not gigantic falls like Niagara, but their height and their sky-blue water make them a breathtaking sight.

The Hualapai Indians live along the South Rim of the Grand Canyon directly west of the Havasupai reservation. They have some forest land—their name means "Pine Tree Folk"—and enough grazing land on their reservation to support a fair-sized cattle operation, which provides them with an income.

The section of Arizona north of the Grand Canyon, and running west from the shores of Lake Powell to the Nevada state line, is known to Arizonans as the Strip Country. This is a sparsely populated area, dominated by sagebrush rather than by people. For many years the inhabitants of the Strip Country identified more with Utah than with Arizona, partly because of their predominantly Mormon background and partly because the Grand Canyon cut them off from the rest of Arizona. Thus they did their trading—and even their voting and a lot of their living—in Utah.

In the Strip Country there is a small city named Fredonia, and it is one of my favorite spots. Fredonia is the place where I have ended every political campaign I have ever run, including my presidential one. The town was

SNOW-MANTLED CHOLLA AND YUCCA, DETRITAL VALLEY

founded by Mormons seeking freedom to practice their religious beliefs, and it is still filled with delightful, freedom-loving religious people.

Pipe Spring National Monument, another point of interest in the strip, also has a Mormon background. The spring itself, which has created an oasis of green around it, was discovered in 1858 by Mormon missionaries to the Hopi. The missionaries were followed by settlers, and in 1870 the Mormon church built a fort, originally called Winsor Castle, to provide protection from Indian raids. The fort became a national monument in 1923. Visitors to Pipe Spring not only can learn how the settlers defended themselves, but also can watch demonstrations of pioneer domestic and ranching skills.

Downstream from Grand Canyon National Park, the flow of the Colorado River has been dammed to better serve human needs for an adequate water supply, protection from floods, and the generation of electric power. The three dams in the Canyon Country—Hoover, Davis, and Parker—also link this part of Arizona to the states of Nevada and California. Hoover Dam, begun in 1931 and finished in 1936, is the most famous of these. Its 726-foot height makes it the highest concrete dam in the United States. The lake created by the dam is one of the world's largest man-made reservoirs—Lake Mead, which is 115 miles long and has over 500 miles of shoreline. It is part of the huge Lake Mead National Recreation Area, whose close to 2 million acres stretch along both the Arizona and Nevada banks of the Colorado River.

Some sixty miles below Hoover Dam is Davis Dam. This dam was authorized in 1941, but World War II delayed its completion until 1950. Primarily designed as a reclamation project, it nevertheless has created a fine man-made lake for boating and fishing—Lake Mohave, which is also part of the Lake Mead National Recreation Area. Still farther downriver, on the Yuma County side of the Mohave-Yuma county line, is Parker Dam, which has created Lake Havasu. Parker Dam was completed in 1941.

Here, along the shores of Lake Havasu, a unique link between the Old World and the New World has been established. Visitors come to the modern American town of Lake Havasu City to view the London Bridge, which was built across the Thames River in London between 1823 and 1831 to replace an older bridge dating from the year 1209. In 1968 the London Bridge was destined to be dismantled and sold, and Robert McCulloch, Sr., the developer of Havasu City, succeeded in purchasing it when his offer of 2,460,000 dollars proved to be the highest bid. The 130,000-ton granite bridge was taken apart carefully, piece by piece, and each piece was numbered

to correspond with the piece next to it. Blueprints were drawn and advanced engineering techniques used to reconstruct the bridge in the Arizona desert. When the bridge was reassembled, there was no water flowing underneath it, but that problem was easily overcome by digging a channel and diverting part of the lake. The bridge now spans an artificial river, called the Little Thames. It was dedicated in October 1971 by the Lord Mayor of London and his retinue.

The area between Davis Dam and Parker Dam offers other places of interest besides the London Bridge. South of Davis Dam is the Fort Mohave Indian Reservation, which runs along the Colorado River for some twenty miles. The fort itself was built in 1859 to protect California-bound immigrants from the Mohave Indians, who were known for their fierce hand-to-hand combat. In 1890, ten years after the reservation was established, the fort was put to use as a school for the Indian children. The religion of the Mohave includes an annual mourning rite in which images of loved ones who died during the past year are burned on a funeral pyre.

Just downstream from Lake Havasu City is Lake Havasu State Park, where one can enjoy water sports, golf, and tennis. And the two sections of the Havasu National Wildlife Refuge are to the north and to the south of the state park.

As a footnote to my discussion of the Canyon Country, I'd like to mention that in the 1850s this part of Arizona was the scene of an experiment in which camels from the Middle East were brought to the desert of the American Southwest to serve as beasts of burden. Edward F. Beale, a lieutenant in the navy, dreamed up the idea, and Secretary of War Jefferson Davis was taken by it. Congress appropriated 30,000 dollars for purchasing the animals, and two shipments of camels arrived in Texas, in 1856 and 1857. The Beale expedition left Camp Verde, Texas, in June 1857 to open a road for westering wagons. Beale led his expedition overland to Santa Fe and then headed west, setting out more or less on what would later become U.S. Highway 66. He reached the Colorado River in January 1858. Beale himself was enthusiastic about "this economical and noble brute," and he used camels again on later expeditions, but Congress ignored his request that 1,000 more camels be purchased. Some of the beasts strayed off into the desert wilderness, and as late as 1920 wild camels could occasionally be spotted wandering around Mohave County. In Quartzsite, Arizona, in Yuma County, there is a monument honoring one of the Arab camel drivers who were brought over to pack and drive the camels.

Above– COLORADO RIVER IN THE EASTERN PART OF GRAND CANYON NATIONAL PARK
Right– MAGIC CANYON DESIGNS, MARBLE CANYON

Left– TOROWEAP POINT (EAST VIEW), *Above–* FOG-SHROUDED SOUTH RIM,
and Below– TOWER AND JUNIPER (SOUTH RIM) IN GRAND CANYON NATIONAL PARK

Left– BRIGHT ANGEL POINT (NORTH RIM),
Above– WINDOW OF LIGHT—ISIS AND BUDDHA TEMPLES,
and Overleaf– DEVA, BRAHMA, AND ZOROASTER TEMPLES IN GRAND CANYON NATIONAL PARK

Left– MOONEY FALLS *and Below–* NAVAJO FALLS IN HAVASU CANYON

HIGH COUNTRY

A<small>N IRREGULAR BELT OF MOUNTAINS CUTS ACROSS ARIZONA ON A NORTHWEST-TO-SOUTHEAST DIAGONAL, DIVIDING THE NORTHERN PLATEAU FROM THE SOUTHERN DESERT. THIS HIGH COUNTRY OFFERS NOT</small> only a wealth of natural beauty and magnificence, but also many places of human interest, both ancient and contemporary. The region abounds in Indian ruins and present-day Indian villages, ghost towns, and thriving cities like Flagstaff and Prescott. The natural beauty of the area is to be found in its mountains, streams, and canyons, in its dense woodlands and its brightly colored, flower-strewn meadows.

The dominant geological feature of the High Country is the Mogollon Rim, or the rim of the Mogollon Plateau. Stretching for more than 200 miles across east-central Arizona, this escarpment, caused by faulting, rises precipitously above the valley floor. In addition to being the outstanding geological formation, the Mogollon Rim, along with the White Mountains to the southeast, is the primary watershed in the area, with streams on the north side of the rim and on the northeastern slopes of the White Mountains draining ultimately into the Little Colorado River, and those on the south side of the rim and the southern and western slopes of the mountains draining into the Gila and Salt rivers.

To stand atop the Mogollon Rim in southern Coconino County and look to the south gives me the feeling that I am high up in an observation tower affording an unrestricted view for miles. Many times on a clear day I have been able to see the distinctive tops of the Four Peaks in the Mazatzal Mountains, over fifty miles away. With a sheer drop of more than 2,000 feet at its highest points, the Mogollon Rim is surely one of Arizona's most scenic wonders. Forests of spruce and fir grow on the higher reaches of the rim, as well as on the White Mountains.

In and around the White Mountains in southern Apache County is some of the world's most beautiful high country, including the spectacular 11,403-foot Baldy Peak. Throughout this entire area, visitors can find charming small towns—such as Nutrioso and Alpine, both located at elevations of some 8,000 feet—that are sur- rounded by soaring mountains covered with spruce, pine, oak, aspen, and maple. In the fall of the year the deciduous trees feel the touch of Jack Frost, and their oranges, browns, reds, and yellows intermix with the deep green of the pines to make a breathtaking scene. It is from here westward, on the Mogollon Plateau north of the rim, that Arizona can lay claim to the largest stand of ponderosa pine in the United States.

Both Nutrioso and Alpine are near the northern end of what is known as the Coronado Trail, the stretch of U.S. Highway 666 between Clifton and Springerville that approximates the route followed by Francisco Vásquez de Coronado in 1540 when he sought the Seven Cities of Cíbola. From Clifton, at an elevation of 3,460 feet, the Coronado Trail winds its way northward, passing through the Apache National Forest. During the course of its journey, the trail rises well above the 10,000-foot mark and travels through what can best be described as pic-ture-postcard country. And the changes in elevation are accompanied by changes in climate. In the early fall of the year, a traveler can start out from the Clifton-Morenci area, which will still be having almost summery weather, and by the time he has reached the small village of Han-nagan Meadow, only forty-five miles to the north but at an elevation of over 9,000 feet, he could easily find him-self in the middle of a winter snowstorm. Fall is the best time to follow the Coronado Trail, for then the trees are resplendent with a whole palette of hues.

The White Mountains form part of the terrain of the Fort Apache Indian Reservation, which, through the industry and enterprise of the White Mountain Apache, has become a summer vacationland for thousands of Arizonans. On the reservation are dozens of well-stocked lakes and streams, both large and small, that appeal not only to the fisherman, but also to the camper and the picnicker on a one-day outing. And just south of the highway from Springerville to McNary, the Apache have developed one of the finest and most modern ski resorts in the country at Sunrise Lake.

Along its southern boundary the Fort Apache reservation adjoins another one for Apache Indians, the San Carlos Indian Reservation. The two reservations represent a considerable land area—almost 3½ million acres altogether. And the Apache living on the two reservations number more than 13,000, which is actually an increase over the number of Apache at the time of the coming of the white man.

The Apache belong to the same language group as the Navajo, and like the Navajo they call themselves the *Dineh,* "the people." *Apache* comes from a Zuñi word meaning "enemy," a reference to the Apache's historic role as raiders and fighters. Today they follow more peaceful pursuits. In addition to developing the resort potential of their lakes and streams, the Apache on both reservations raise cattle from top bloodlines and harvest some of the timber that grows on the slopes of their mountains, being careful not to take too much at one time. The San Carlos Apache are beginning to make hand-crafted jewelry from the beautiful yellow-green peridot gemstones found on their reservation. And they are reaping benefits from a shrub that grows on their land, the jojoba, whose seeds yield a liquid wax that can be used instead of whale oil in candles, cosmetics, and pharmaceutical products.

The religion of the Apache centers around natural features that play a vital role in their lives, such as the sun, the moon, and the mountains.

National forest land nearly encircles the two Apache reservations. The Apache National Forest is to the east; the Sitgreaves to the north, on the other side of the Mogollon Rim; the Tonto to the west; and a small section of the Coronado National Forest to the south. And they are traversed by a number of rivers fed by mountain streams. One of the most important of these is the Salt River, formed on the wooded slopes of the White Mountains by the confluence of the White and Black rivers. (The water of the Salt actually has a salty taste, especially when the river is low, because several large salt springs feed into it.) The Salt has carved a deep, winding canyon in the course of its westward flow. Located on the west-central boundary of the Apache's land, the Salt River Canyon is the most awe-inspiring sight along the river.

The Salt River is the major tributary of the Gila, which it joins farther west. The Gila River cuts across the southern part of the San Carlos reservation, where it has been dammed to form San Carlos Lake. Though it may contain scant water during dry spells, the lake is used to irrigate the surrounding farmlands.

Coolidge Dam, which created San Carlos Lake, was dedicated by President Calvin Coolidge in 1930. One of the problems connected with building the dam was that it would flood the Apache's tribal burial ground. The Apache were strongly opposed to disinterring the bodies of their forefathers, and finally concrete was poured over the burial ground to form a slab that stands between the graves and the water.

Some of the towns near the San Carlos reservation, in the southeastern part of Arizona's High Country, are known for their mines. Gold and silver were mined here at one time, and there are some large asbestos mines, but the area is primarily a source of copper. One of the most important copper-mining towns is Globe, just west of the San Carlos reservation. Globe was named after the Globe Mine, a large silver deposit that was discovered

there in 1873. Though silver lured the first settlers to Globe, it was the Old Dominion copper mine that brought about its heyday. The mines are not as productive as they once were, but the people are staying, instead of leaving, for the town's beautiful location and the rugged Pinal Mountains just to the south are ideal settings for retirement living. A sister city of Globe is Miami, which owes its development to the Miami Copper Company. And just northwest of Miami is Inspiration, another copper-mining town. Actually, the three cities almost meld into one, and the great majority of the non-Indians in Gila County live in and around them.

To the east of the San Carlos reservation, in Greenlee County, is the copper-mining town of Morenci. Founded in the early 1880s, Morenci is the site of a copper mine with two open pits, one of them among the largest in the United States. Both pits may be seen from a lookout on U.S. Highway 666 and it is well worth stopping to take a look, if only to marvel at the engineering ability that could create something on this scale.

South of the San Carlos reservation, in Graham County, is a striking natural landmark—10,713-foot-high Mount Graham, which can be seen from many places in the southern part of Arizona. Its slopes ascend through a series of climatic zones, and it is capped with deep snow in the winter.

Throughout Graham County, there are many historic places that serve as reminders of the struggles between the white man and the Indian. Two such places are Fort Grant and Fort Thomas. Fort Grant was established in late 1872 or early 1873 as a substitute for the old and unhealthy Camp Grant. Located on a broad, grassy step of the southern slope of Mount Graham, it was an ideal post because of its 5,000-foot elevation and its central location along a number of Indian trails. Some of the original buildings are being used today as part of a state vocational school for delinquent boys.

The other post, Fort Thomas, is located close to the Gila River just upstream from the San Carlos reservation. Like many other early military posts, Fort Thomas had a checkered beginning, and not until 1884 were funds allocated to erect permanent buildings. But its end began just two short years later, with the surrender of Geronimo, and in 1892 it was abandoned by the army. Today the fort is the site of a high school devoted primarily to the Apache Indians, and it also houses the Indian Health Service and other government agencies.

The Gila River has always been a prime factor in the settlement and development of this area, from the time of the earliest Indians to the present. The stretch of the river south of the San Carlos reservation, between the Gila Mountains and the Pinaleno Mountains, has been used since about 1872 to irrigate the crops grown in the rich agricultural region around it, known as the Safford Valley. This valley is one of the major producers of long-staple cotton, one of the best types for making fine cotton cloth. In the spring and summer, a journey through the Safford Valley reveals the beauty—as well as the efficiency—of the American farmer's handiwork. Another important product of the valley is its fine cattle.

Most of the people in the Safford Valley are farmers

or ranchers, and the majority of them are Mormons. Thanks to this Mormon background, there are excellent examples here of what has become known as Mormon architecture. While not fancy, the homes built to this standard have a distinctive flair and are soon easily recognized even by the novice. Because of the migratory route of the Mormons from Utah to Mexico by way of the eastern side of Arizona, several different Mormon communities can be found in this part of the state.

Like the Safford Valley, the Tonto Basin is bounded by mountain ranges. Located west of the Apache reservations and forming part of Tonto National Forest, the Tonto Basin is sandwiched between the Sierra Ancha and the Mazatzal Mountains. It widens like a big horn, with the smallest part at Theodore Roosevelt Lake and the largest part facing the Mogollon Rim. Some unusually rough country is contained within the basin, and it was once an Indian stronghold. (Its name comes from the phrase *Tonto Apache,* or "foolish Apache," which nineteenth-century writers indiscriminately applied to all the Indians living in the area.)

In the Tonto Basin are a number of little towns with intriguing names, such as Pine, Strawberry, and Payson. The town of Payson is the center of a growing population of retired people, and it also attracts a large group who travel north from the hot valleys of the desert to spend their summers in its cool woodlands. One of the attractions of the Payson area is Zane Grey's cabin, where Grey stayed for a while when he came to Arizona in 1908 to gather material for the Western stories that made him famous. In fact, one of his better-known novels is called *Under the Tonto Rim.* Another attraction is a nearby rock formation, the Tonto Natural Bridge, which is the world's largest natural bridge. Through a hole in the massive travertine bridge can be seen the gorge far below. This natural wonder was once owned by a Scotsman named David Gowan, who planted an orchard on its surface.

While that part of the High Country south of the Mogollon Rim offers many points of great interest and beauty, such as the White Mountains, the two Apache reservations, and the Tonto Basin, the section of the High Country north of the rim is hardly second to it in either quality. No fewer than four of Arizona's national monuments are in the northern part of the High Country—Montezuma Castle, Tuzigoot, Walnut Canyon, and Sunset Crater. Montezuma Castle National Monument, established in 1906, is some thirty-seven miles northwest of Payson, in the Verde Valley. The national monument protects cliff dwellings that were built out of river boulders and chunks of limestone on a cliff overlooking Beaver Creek during the thirteenth and fourteenth centuries. Montezuma Castle itself is a five-story dwelling with twenty rooms. A nearby structure called Castle A is considerably larger but not as well preserved. These "apartment houses" were probably erected by the Sinagua Indians, who moved into the Verde Valley about 1100 A.D. from an area farther north. Seven miles northeast of Montezuma Castle is Montezuma Well, a limestone sinkhole containing a fifty-five-foot-deep lake. There are more Indian pueblos around the sinkhole. The name

69

Montezuma comes from the mistaken belief of the early white settlers that these ruins were at one time the dwellings of the Aztec Indians.

Tuzigoot, about eighteen miles to the northwest in the same valley, became a national monument in 1939, following its excavation by University of Arizona archaeologists in 1933–1934. This national monument is similar to Montezuma Castle in many ways, since it too protects what remains of a town built by the Sinagua Indians. The archaeologists discovered that the Sinagua buried their dead infants in the walls or beneath the floors of the rooms, perhaps believing that their souls would be reincarnated in the next children born there.

Walnut Canyon National Monument, thirty-eight miles northeast of Tuzigoot, is yet a third memorial to the lives of the ancient Indians who once populated this part of Arizona. They built more than 300 cliff rooms in the limestone walls of Walnut Canyon, which afforded them protection from the elements and from enemy tribes, a source of water in Walnut Creek, and fertile soil for growing crops within two miles of the canyon rims. Lieutenant Edward Beale viewed the Walnut Canyon ruins in 1858. By the end of the century they had been subjected to serious vandalism, which led to the establishment of Walnut Canyon National Monument in 1915.

I mentioned Sunset Crater National Monument in connection with the Indian Country because of its close link with the Indians who once lived at Wupatki, but technically it belongs to Arizona's High Country. The ancient Indians may have left the Sunset Crater region where they used to live because the fertile soil created by the eruption of the volcano brought such an influx of other Indians that the overcrowding became too much for them, and they set out on the exodus that produced the cliff dwellings at Walnut Canyon, Tuzigoot, and Montezuma Castle. An interesting contemporary sidelight about Sunset Crater National Monument is that the American astronauts and the photographic experts of NASA did their training in its vicinity so they would be acquainted with the type of terrain they would find on the moon. The lava mountain got its name from Major John Wesley Powell, who was reminded of a sunset when he saw the spectrum of colors on its side.

In addition to its four national monuments, the stretch of the High Country north of the Mogollon Rim is the location of one of Arizona's most interesting cities—Flagstaff, which is fondly nicknamed "Flag" by Arizonans. According to popular legend, Flagstaff received its name in 1876 when a contingent of scouts awaiting westbound settlers made a flagpole by trimming all the limbs from a pine tree to celebrate the Fourth of July, and it has been called Flagstaff ever since. This delightful city of more than 32,000 people is nestled at the southern foot of San Francisco Mountain at an altitude of 6,970 feet above sea level, which gives it cool weather during the summer and cold weather with some heavy snows during the winter.

Because of its central location to all the Indian tribes of northern Arizona, Flagstaff sometimes resembles a mini-United Nations of Indians. On Saturday afternoons it is not uncommon to see Indian people in their distinctive garb going about their errands. But the greatest gathering of Indians in Flagstaff can be seen every year around the Fourth of July, when the city hosts the Southwest Indian Powwow. This colorful three-day celebration attracts thousands of Indians from throughout the Southwest, and many non-Indians, with its parades, dances, and rodeos. And the Museum of Northern Arizona, just outside of Flagstaff, has exhibits that provide insight into early Indian cultures as well as contemporary Indian life.

One of the most important cultural centers in Flagstaff is Northern Arizona University. Founded in 1899 as Northern Arizona Normal School, the university now has more than 11,000 students. Its campus is the scene of the annual Flagstaff Summer Festival, a potpourri of films, plays, concerts, and art exhibits. The Northern Arizona Pioneers' Historical Museum illuminates the history of early settlers in the area. And for those with a scientific bent, the Lowell Observatory, through whose telescope the planet Pluto was discovered in 1930, offers tours and shows.

Flagstaff's chief natural attraction, which can be seen from many places in Arizona, is San Francisco Mountain to the north. Because it has three separate peaks—Agassiz Peak, Fremont Peak, and 12,633-foot Humphreys Peak, the highest point in Arizona—San Francisco Mountain is commonly referred to as the San Francisco Peaks. The first white men to see the mountain were probably those in the Coronado expedition, and it was referred to by several other early Spanish explorers. It was eventually named after Saint Francis of Assisi by the Franciscan fathers at Oraibi. The peaks themselves were once centers of volcanic activity. A good time of year to see San Francisco Mountain at its most spectacular is during the autumn, when the cold evening air begins to bring a rainbow of color to its hillsides. The mountain is in the Coconino National Forest, which completely surrounds the Flagstaff area.

Just a few miles south of Flagstaff is the beginning of a deep, rugged side canyon of the Mogollon Rim called Oak Creek Canyon. Looking down over Oak Creek from atop the plateau, a person can see one of the most beautiful examples of nature's handiwork. In some ways, Oak Creek Canyon is more appealing than the Grand Canyon; since it is so much smaller, it has a much more intimate feeling. Parts of the canyon floor are overgrown with wild flowers, including bluebells, columbines, and Indian paintbrushes. With its sheer walls and the vivid red of its wind-and-water-eroded formations, Oak Creek Canyon has become a natural magnet for those who love the outdoors, and the excellent fishing in Oak Creek has attracted many an angler. Many Westerns have been filmed in the Oak Creek Canyon area, and it is probably the setting of Grey's *Call of the Canyon*.

In the western part of the High Country is a town that played a major role during Arizona's territorial days—Prescott, now a sizable community of more than 14,000 people. Perched on mountainous terrain at the edge of the western unit of the Prescott National Forest, Prescott is known as The Mile-High City, though its elevation is actually slightly higher than a mile above sea level.

Prescott was Arizona's first territorial capital. The man appointed to be governor of Arizona Territory, John

N. Goodwin, took his oath of office on December 29, 1863, at the first place where he felt certain that he was on Arizona soil—this was at Navajo Springs in Apache County—then moved on to Fort Whipple. After a few months' stay at the fort, the governor and his retinue established themselves in what was to become the city of Prescott, where the First Territorial Legislature met in September 1864. Named after historian William Hickling Prescott, who wrote the classic *Conquest of Mexico,* the site seemed to be an ideal place for the capital because of its central location and because of the diverse economic interests represented there. But other considerations proved to be stronger than these, and Tucson became the territorial capital in 1867. Though Prescott was reinstated as the capital in 1877, it had to relinquish the honor to Phoenix in 1889.

Despite its vicissitudes as territorial capital, Prescott grew to be quite a robust town, as Western towns were supposed to be. The descriptions of Prescott's activities given me by my father and uncle, who lived there during the town's infancy, lead me to believe that the "wild and woolly" aspects of the place might have been exaggerated—but then my uncle was the town's mayor for many years. The town did not attract much attention until movies and popular novels started to appear about the wild, wild West.

Prescott is still an interesting old Western community, much as it was in the days when Arizona first became a territory. The street that runs along the west side of the plaza became known as Whiskey Row because at one time every building in the block was a saloon. The main part of town is dominated by a large courthouse built in the center of a pretty little park, and in front of the courthouse stands an equestrian statue of William "Bucky" O'Neill, the first Arizonan to enlist for the Spanish-American War, who fought as a Rough Rider and was killed in the Battle of San Juan Hill. (When Teddy Roosevelt needed stalwart recruits for the Rough Riders, he appealed to the governor of Arizona Territory as well as to those of New Mexico and Oklahoma. Arizona contributed three troops to the Rough Riders.) O'Neill's nickname came from the fact that he was continually "bucking the tiger" at the faro game in the Palace Hotel, on the west side of the courthouse square.

In 1888 Prescott hosted the first public rodeo ever held in the United States, and the event, known as the Prescott Frontier Days Rodeo, has been held yearly since that time. In addition to that attraction, since 1920 a quasi-Indian ceremonial has been put on every year by non-Indians who call themselves "Smoki"—not an Indian name, though it sounds like one. In August, on the Saturday nearest the full moon, the men and women of the Smoki group perform exact replicas of the Southwest Indians' ceremonies, songs, and dances. The Smoki also maintain a beautiful museum in Prescott, where visitors can see the collection of rugs, baskets, bowls, and other Indian artifacts put together by the members of this organization. The museum also houses a library of Indian history and photographs.

While the Smoki Museum preserves part of Arizona's Indian past, the Sharlot Hall Museum and Old Governor's Mansion preserve part of Arizona's territorial past, complete with furniture and household utensils from the frontier era. Prescott truly embodies a rich cultural heritage. For a person visiting the state for the first time, this is an ideal Western town to spend some time in, with friendly people and a climate that is cool in the summer and a little cold in the winter, but always livable.

The western stretch of the High Country does not have any Indian reservations comparable in size to the Fort Apache and San Carlos reservations to the east, but it does have two small ones—the Yavapai Indian Reservation, just north of Prescott, and the Camp Verde Indian Reservation, some thirty miles farther east. On the Yavapai reservation live about 100 Yavapai Indians, while the Camp Verde reservation is home for over 800 Yavapai-Apache. The Yavapai once roamed over vast territories in Arizona, but many of them died of tuberculosis after they were settled on reservations.

The Camp Verde Indian Reservation is divided into two small sections, one to the north and one to the south of the town of Camp Verde. This town began in late 1865 as an army post called Camp Lincoln, which served as a supply depot and the main jumping-off point for military expeditions against the hostile Indians who roamed the area. The installation was renamed Camp Verde in 1868 because of an army policy that two posts could not have the same name. Today the townspeople have got together to save and restore as much of the old camp as possible, and it is well worth taking the time to visit.

One of the outstanding natural features of the western part of the High Country is the Verde River, which rises in the hills north of Prescott. Fed by Sycamore Creek, Oak Creek, West Clear Creek, Fossil Creek, and finally the East Verde River, it winds its way southeast to meet the Salt River. The Verde itself begins its journey up in Chino Valley, a wide, beautiful, grassy meadowland of rolling hills. As it begins its path southward, it drops through the Verde Canyon and then out into the Verde Valley, passing by Tuzigoot National Monument. Outlining the west side of the Verde Valley at this point is Mingus Mountain. High up on the side of that mountain is the historic city of Jerome. Once a large copper-mining community, Jerome is now one of the most picturesque ghost towns in the United States. It is being rehabilitated and redecorated by a group of artistic-minded people who are attracted by its breathtaking views and distinctive architecture.

The Bradshaw Mountains extend south from Prescott for thirty or forty miles, rising in places to some 9,000 feet. These mountains are crisscrossed with deep rugged side canyons, and they support an almost impenetrable growth of cedar, oak, and pine. During the winter, a person can be sailing on the clear, blue waters of Lake Pleasant, just south of the Bradshaws, and look up to see the mountains wearing a beautiful white mantle of snow. It was in and around the Bradshaws that the Arizona "gold fever" struck the hardest. One of the mining camps grew into a town with a population of about 5,000, which was a factor in the choice of Prescott nearby as the first territorial capital.

Left– SUNRISE AT HAWLEY LAKE
and Above– THE LITTLE COLORADO RIVER'S HEADWATERS IN THE WHITE MOUNTAINS
Below– GRAND FALLS OF THE LITTLE COLORADO RIVER

73

Above– HEADWATERS OF THE WHITE RIVER, FORT APACHE INDIAN RESERVATION
Right– SUNFLOWERS IN BLACK RIVER COUNTRY, WHITE MOUNTAINS

74

Left– LUPINES AND POPPIES ON MOUNT TURNBULL, SAN CARLOS INDIAN RESERVATION
Above– PRICKLY PEARS ABOVE SALT RIVER CANYON
Below– CASCADE, SALT RIVER CANYON
Overleaf– OAK CREEK CANYON AT DAWN

Above– MOGOLLON RIM *Below–* PREHISTORIC PUEBLO,
TUZIGOOT NATIONAL MONUMENT *Right–* MONTEZUMA CASTLE,
MONTEZUMA CASTLE NATIONAL MONUMENT

VALLEY of the SUN

TODAY ARIZONA'S POPULATION IS ABOUT 80 PERCENT URBAN, AND A SIZABLE PORTION OF THIS 80 PERCENT IS CLUSTERED IN THE SALT RIVER VALLEY, AN AREA THAT HAS COME TO BE KNOWN AS THE VALLEY OF THE SUN. THE largest city in the Valley of the Sun—and in all of Arizona—is Phoenix, the state capital. Other cities in the region include Scottsdale, Glendale, Mesa, Tempe, and Sun City, which was developed as a retirement community. As its name implies, the Valley of the Sun attracts many people, both old and young, by virtue of its warm, sunny climate and the carefree life-style made possible by balmy days. The preponderance of sunny days and the dearth of rainfall might be reason enough to classify much of this area as desert, but human ingenuity has made it a hospitable and enjoyable place to live by harnessing the precious water of the Salt River.

Not only is the Salt River used for irrigation today, thanks to modern engineering techniques, but it was used in a comparable way centuries ago by earlier inhabitants of the valley, the Hohokam Indians. The Hohokam had come, as others had before and after them, because of the availability of water, and they built a canal system more than 600 miles in extent. Some of the present-day canals actually follow the lines of the old Indian canals and ditches. The very name *Phoenix* is a tribute to the Hohokam civilization that once throve in the Valley of the Sun; just as the phoenix of classical mythology was born anew out of its own ashes, so the city of Phoenix was built on the "ashes" of an earlier people. *Hohokam* itself means "The People Who Have Gone," and it was probably a drying up of their water supply that caused them to leave the Salt River Valley.

The availability of water was a vital consideration in the founding and the development of Phoenix, just as it was a factor in keeping the Hohokam village going for so many years. In 1867, when prospector Jack Swilling of Wickenburg came riding into the Salt River Valley around the north end of the White Tank Mountains, he noticed the richness of the soil turned up by his horse's hooves. Water—that was all this land ever needed. He also noted a regular pattern of depressions leading from the Salt River. Further exploration revealed what was left of the Hohokam canals, which strengthened Swilling's belief in the feasibility of irrigated farming in the valley. He organized the Swilling Irrigation Canal Company and moved into the Salt River Valley, where he commenced the task of excavating the old canals to divert some of the Salt River water onto the land.

The small agricultural community that developed as settlers moved in to avail themselves of the irrigated farmland was first called Pumpkinville, in honor of one of their staple crops. But in 1870 the settlers felt a need for a more dignified name, and a meeting was called to find one. Swilling, who had been a Confederate soldier, wanted to name the new settlement Stonewall after the famous general, while others suggested the name Salina, after the Salt River. Neither of these two caught the fancy of the settlers. Finally an Englishman named Darrel Duppa, who was one of the canal builders, suggested that Phoenix would be an appropriate name for the new town, since it would spring from the ruins of a former civilization.

The town of Phoenix was surveyed and laid out by Captain William Hancock, whose daughter was my sixth-grade teacher. In January of 1871 the *Prescott Miner* advertised "A great sale of lots at Phoenix, Arizona." Sixty-one of the lots were sold in this first effort at an average price of forty-three dollars each. The first lot sold was at the southwest corner of First Street and Washington, and the buyer got it for what was then a steep price of 116 dollars. Today, the lot would cost millions of dollars. By 1875 there were sixteen saloons and four dance halls in the town. The fourth of July 1887 brought the first Southern Pacific train from Maricopa Wells, and this was one of the most important events in the history of Phoenix. Another great event came in 1889, when the city was made the territorial capital. And the early growth of the town brought the Santa Fe Railway in 1895.

More than half of all Arizonans live in the Phoenix metropolitan area. When the city was incorporated in 1881, it had about 1,700 people. By the time of my birth in Phoenix in 1909, there were some 10,000 people living here, and by now the population of the city proper has mushroomed to more than 700,000 and that of the metropolitan area to well over a million.

Given such statistics of growth, it is obvious that the influx of settlers to the Valley of the Sun was not halted by the passing of the frontier. On the contrary, more than half a million Americans have immigrated to Arizona's Sonoran Desert—mainly to the Phoenix and Tucson areas —within the past ten years, some seeking a more healthful climate or an exciting retirement community, some attracted by the recreational activities, and others drawn by the many business opportunities. And while Tucson has a substantial number of citizens who urge controlled growth—in view of increasing pollution, water problems, and the general threat posed by an expanding population to the delicate desert ecology—most of the citizens of Phoenix are advocates of expansion. This is one of the reasons why I believe that within my lifetime Phoenix, now the thirteenth largest city in the United States, will rise in rank to the fifth or sixth largest city.

The Phoenix area is a major resort center. Among its recreational attractions are horseback riding, golf, tennis, and a variety of water sports—fishing, swimming, and boating. Some of the most popular spots for boating and fishing are a short distance north of Phoenix—Lake Pleasant, Bartlett Reservoir, and Horseshoe Recreational Area.

Other attractions in the Phoenix area include the Heard Museum of Anthropology and Primitive Arts, to which I gave my collection of kachina dolls; the Phoenix Art Museum, which houses the Arizona Costume Institute; and Arizona State University, with more than 30,000 students, in nearby Tempe. Pioneer Arizona, north of Phoenix, captures the spirit of the Old West in a re-created frontier town. For animal lovers there are the Phoenix Zoo and the Tropic Gardens Zoo, and for plant lovers there is the Desert Botanical Garden, where visitors can enjoy 150 acres of the world's desert flora and where those who come in February can see the cactus show. Every January, Phoenix hosts the Arizona National Livestock Show, and during the first two weeks of November it is the scene of the colorful Arizona State Fair.

While the phenomenal growth of the Phoenix area has helped give impetus to a wealth of recreational, cultural, and business opportunities, it has also placed great demands on the water supply, necessitating an increasingly sophisticated system of canals and dams. The Salt River Valley has come a long way since Jack Swilling chanced upon the Hohokam canals a century ago.

Following severe drought conditions in the late 1890s, farmers in the valley were forced to recognize the need for a better water distribution system than their canals were providing. In 1902 Theodore Roosevelt signed a Reclamation Act permitting the construction of dams on rivers to irrigate arid land. It was obvious to those who lived in the Valley of the Sun that more water had to be supplied to keep them from going the way of the Hohokam. Consequently, the first stone in a large masonry dam was laid on September 20, 1906. Five years later, when the structure was completed, it was dedicated by the man whose signature had made its existence possible—Theodore Roosevelt. Originally named Tonto Dam, it was renamed in his honor in 1959. In addition to serving as a reservoir for irrigation, the twenty-three-mile-long Theodore Roosevelt Lake created by the dam offers some of the best fishing and boating found anywhere in the state.

Theodore Roosevelt Dam stands at the junction of Tonto Creek, which has its origin on the Mogollon Rim, and the Salt River. Below the dam, three others have been built, creating Apache Lake, Canyon Lake, and Saguaro Lake. Below Saguaro Lake, the Salt River receives the water of the Verde River, whose flow is intercepted by Horseshoe and Bartlett dams to further impound water for central Arizona. And below the junction of the Verde and the Salt is Granite Reef Dam, a diversion dam that channels water into the big canals on the south side of the valley and into the main canal, the Arizona Canal, on the north side. Off of these large canals that bound the Valley of the Sun flow laterals, and off of the laterals flow the ditches that irrigate the lands of the farmers.

This very complex system of irrigation is run by the owners of the land under the name of the Salt River Project. They, in turn, provide electricity generated by the power plants and sell it outside of the central area of the valley. Despite this elaborate irrigation system, farming is rather rapidly disappearing from the Salt River Valley, and within a relatively few years it will probably still be practiced only in the southern and the far western ends of the valley.

The outlying areas of the Valley of the Sun offer points of interest as compelling as those of the Phoenix metropolitan area. And an excellent way of reaching some of the outlying points is via the Apache Trail, or Arizona Highway 88, a semicircular route that runs between Apache Junction and Globe, passing through the Superstition Mountains east of Phoenix. The Apache Trail skirts Canyon Lake, Theodore Roosevelt Lake, and Tonto National Monument, winding around the caves and gorges created by the streams flowing into the Salt River.

Just east of Apache Junction, the Apache Trail traverses the Superstition Mountains, which were called *Sierra de la Espuma*—"Mountains of Foam"—by the Spanish because a broad white streak resembling the froth of waves cuts across the limestone of their face. The Superstition Mountains are believed to be the location of the legendary Lost Dutchman Mine, which is the most famous "lost mine" in Arizona's folklore. According to the legend, a young Mexican lover sought refuge from the anger of his girl friend's father in the Superstition Mountains. There he found a rich deposit of gold, and he returned home to bring back friends who could help him carry away the precious metal. As they started off with the gold, all but two of his party—both small boys—were ambushed and killed by the Apache. The boys returned to the mine with a partner when they grew up, but just as they began to dig, a Dutchman with a long white beard appeared. Told about the gold deposit, the Dutchman killed the three Mexicans and took possession of the mine. He later killed eight more prospectors, including his nephew, who were looking for his mine. And the secret of the mine's whereabouts died with the Dutchman.

Running more or less parallel to the man-made lakes created by damming the Salt River, the Apache Trail goes by Tonto National Monument just south of Theodore Roosevelt Lake. Like the other national monuments in this part of Arizona, Tonto preserves what has been left behind by an early Indian culture. The Indians who erected the three villages of cliff dwellings now protected as a monument were a Pueblo group known as the Salado. In the early 1300s, after living along the edge of the Salt River for three centuries, they built these cliff dwellings on ridgetops high above the river—probably for better security. Here they lived for about 100 years. Made of stone and mud, the dwellings are three stories high in some places. Like the Hohokam Indians, the Salado built irrigation canals to bring water from the Salt River to their crops, but the ruins of their canals have been covered by Theodore Roosevelt Lake. One of the crops they grew was cotton, which they dyed and wove into beautiful fabrics for making clothing and for trading to other tribes. The Salado were excellent weavers of cotton, as the artifacts found at Tonto National Monument can prove. Tonto has been a national monument since 1907.

Casa Grande National Monument, some thirty-eight miles southeast of Phoenix in the Gila Valley, was established in 1918. The ruins at Casa Grande were once the buildings used by a community of Hohokam Indians, who lived in the Gila and Salt valleys from before the time of Christ to about 1450 A.D. Already mentioned in connection with their outstanding canal system, the Hohokam were advanced in other ways as well—they used acid to etch their artworks, and they played a type of ball game with a rubber ball in a clay arena. The "Casa Grande" itself, built around 1350, is an impressive adobe structure, four stories high in the center and three elsewhere, made from desert soil with a high lime content. The function served by this building remains something of a mystery—probably it was used for ceremonial purposes. In the upper chamber there are seven small apertures aimed at the sky. These were apparently used to

THEODORE ROOSEVELT DAM OVERFLOW

"read" the stars as a way of determining the best planting times. The people in the surrounding villages lived in individual single-room houses, some of which have been excavated, and the entire community was once enclosed by walls, with ladders being the only means of access. The first non-Indian to see Casa Grande was Father Kino, who discovered—and named—the ruins in 1694.

Twenty miles south of Phoenix on the Gila River Indian Reservation, is the Hohokam-Pima archaeological site, which includes some of the remains of the Hohokam irrigation canal system. Though Hohokam-Pima was authorized as a national monument in 1972, and is shown as such on many maps, it is not yet open to the public.

Other traces of the Hohokam civilization that once populated the Valley of the Sun can be found in the Phoenix metropolitan area. Just east of Phoenix is the Park of the Four Waters, containing ruins of another section of the Hohokam's irrigation system. Nearby is Pueblo Grande Ruin. A thriving village centuries ago, Pueblo Grande was excavated by archaeologists from the Smithsonian Institution in the 1930s and 1940s. Among the structures they uncovered was a ball court, further evidence of the Hohokam's interest in games.

While Tonto and Casa Grande national monuments bear witness to the skills and interests of the early Indians who inhabited the Salt and Gila valleys, the four Indian reservations clustered around Phoenix—the Salt River and Fort McDowell reservations to the east and the Gila River and Ak-Chin reservations to the south—testify to the present-day vitality of Indian life in the vicinity of the Valley of the Sun.

The Salt River Indian Community stretches along the Salt River east of Scottsdale. The 49,294-acre reservation is home to some 2,800 Pima and Maricopa Indians. About one-third of the land is being cultivated, with the help of irrigation, and quite a few of the Indians are employed in various industries on the reservation, including a large sand and rock company. The Pima Indians are believed to be descendants of the Hohokam. The early Pima constructed houses in the Salt River Valley similar to those of the Hohokam and also built canals to irrigate their fields, but much of their civilization was destroyed by Apache raids in the seventeenth century. The Maricopa Indians, related to the Yuma, came to live among the Pima in the eighteenth century, following a break with the Yuma. They were able to coexist peacefully with the Pima, though neither tribe could understand the other's language, and the Pima came to their aid when the Yuma attacked them in 1857.

Adjoining the Salt River Indian Community, and about half its size, is the Fort McDowell Indian Reservation, where some 350 Yavapai and Yavapai-Apache Indians live. Because of the reservation's proximity to the rapidly growing Phoenix metropolitan area, it will soon be enclosed by housing developments on three sides. Fort McDowell itself, located within the boundaries of the reservation, was one of the most important military posts in the Southwest. Established as Camp McDowell in 1865, it was used as a base from which to launch expeditions against the Apache.

South of Phoenix is the Gila River Indian Reservation, with some 8,400 Pima and Maricopa Indians living on or near its 371,933 acres. Situated in the Gila River Valley, the reservation is dominated by the gently sloping valley floor. Thanks to the development of three industrial parks on their land, many of the Indians are now employed in light factory work, and about 20 percent of the reservation is being irrigated for agricultural use. In 1969 the Gila River reservation was selected to participate in the Model Cities Program, which provided grants for restructuring the tribal government to make it more responsive to the needs of its constituents.

The Ak-Chin Indian Community, south of the Gila River reservation, sustains a small population of some 260 Papago Indians on its 21,840 acres. Ak-Chin Farm, a tribal enterprise, employs more than half of the reservation's labor force. A falling water table has reduced the acreage that can be cultivated, and the Indians are striving to develop methods of farming that will conserve water.

With its Indian reservations, national monuments, and wild mountainous terrain along the Apache Trail, the Valley of the Sun has much to offer in addition to the attractions of the Phoenix metropolitan area. For those who yearn for a complete change of pace from the city, the Aravaipa Canyon Primitive Area, some seventy miles southeast of Phoenix, preserves the wilderness spirit that prevailed throughout the state before the coming of the white man. The seven-and-a-half-mile-long gorge carved into the rock by the swirling waters of Aravaipa Creek was designated as a primitive area in 1969, so that here present-day Americans can recapture the wonder felt by the first white men ever to set foot in this realm of great natural beauty.

The water of Aravaipa Creek flows year-round—a remarkable phenomenon in the desert—sustaining growths of willows, sycamores, cottonwoods, and ash trees along its banks. More than 150 species of birds have been spotted in the canyon, and after sundown coyotes and mule deer come to drink from the creek. Aravaipa Canyon is an ideal place for horseback riding and hiking, but I would not recommend it for fearful souls. Hikers should wear sturdy shoes, carry a snakebite kit, and check the weather forecast to make sure that no flash floods are imminent. Yet the possibility of danger only adds an aura of authenticity to the wilderness experience.

SUMMER SUNSET OVER CANYON LAKE

Overleaf– SPRINGTIME CHOLLA COLONY
and Above– SAGUAROS IN SUPERSTITION MOUNTAINS
Right– PHOENIX SKYLINE

98

DESERT COUNTRY

THE SOUTHWESTERN SECTION OF ARIZONA CAN BEST BE CALLED THE DESERT COUNTRY, FOR THE RAINFALL HERE IS AS SPARSE AS THE POPULATION. BUT IT WOULD BE MISLEADING TO IMPLY THAT THE WORD *DESERT* SUMS UP the entire region. There are also canyons and mountains and green farmlands along the Colorado River. The area's importance as a source of gold contributed to its major role in the history of the frontier, and it has a special significance for me because of my family's roots in Yuma County.

The Desert Country includes all of Yuma County, along with sections of Maricopa and Pima counties. A considerable part of the land in the region belongs to the federal government and certain sections of it are not open to the public—people driving through it must not leave the right-of-way on the main-traveled roads posted with warning signs. The federal land is used for military purposes and for the protection of wildlife.

The arid terrain that dominates the Desert Country forms part of the Sonoran Desert, which covers some 120,000 square miles in southwestern Arizona, southeastern California, and two Mexican states—Baja California and Sonora. For many, many miles along the Arizona-Mexico border there is nothing to stop a person from going across the border either way. The Spaniards journeying to California across this desolate area traveled along what became known as the Devil's Highway, or sometimes the Highway of Death, because so many emigrants died en route. This country is Arizona desert at its best (or worst)—flat, with an abundance of cacti of all descriptions, and difficult to travel through because of the absence of trails or roads.

Though cacti grow in abundance in the Sonoran Desert, they are nonetheless protected by Arizona's Native Plant Law, under which a "cactus rustler" can receive a maximum penalty of a 1,000-dollar fine for each plant stolen and a year in jail. Even so, rustlers make off with an estimated 25,000 of the stately saguaro cacti each year and sell them to landscapers, who pay up to 400 dollars for a single plant.

Many spots in southwestern Arizona offer unbroken vistas of desert terrain, but one of the best places to ap-preciate the stark beauty of desert plant life is Organ Pipe Cactus National Monument, on the Mexican border in western Pima County. This national monument, established in 1937, is the largest in the state. It protects the organ-pipe cactus, a species rare in the United States, along with other forms of desert vegetation, including the Mexican poppy and magenta owl clover. Its 516 square miles include trails for hikers and two scenic drives: the Ajo Mountain Drive runs along some of the more spectacular stands of the organ-pipe cactus, whose clustered stems sometimes reach a height of twenty feet, and the Puerto Blanco Drive goes by senita cacti in the Senita Basin. And the area is interesting for historical as well as botanical reasons. It was traversed by gold seekers as well as Spaniards bound for California, and later it became the home of miners and ranchers.

Many people were drawn to Arizona's Desert Country by the lure of the precious metals buried beneath the ground. Gold has been found in almost every part of Yuma County, and naturally, it attracted gold seekers from all over the world. One of the most famous of these was named Herman Ehrenberg, a talented mining engineer from Germany who fought for Texas independence and later traveled to Arizona Territory, mapping the country as he went. His maps, drawn over a hundred years ago, are almost as accurate as the maps of today. The Colorado River port of Ehrenberg, now virtually a ghost town, was named in his honor by its founders—my grandfather, who knew him well, and my great-uncle. He had surveyed a large part of the area before being killed in California, probably by Indians.

Other virtual ghost towns in the vicinity that were associated with the gold boom are La Paz and Quartzsite. Placer gold was discovered at La Paz in the early 1860s, and the settlement flourished both as a mining town and as a river port for about seven years. Quartzsite, known today mainly for the monument on the grave of the camel driver connected with the Beale expedition, was once a mining camp and a stage stop. Incidentally, some of Beale's camels ended up in the hands of miners, either as pack animals or as meat. And the camel driver himself, Hadji Ali, known to the locals as "Hi Jolly," developed a fondness for the Arizona desert and prospected in this area after spending several years employed as a camel packer and scout by the army.

While some of the mining towns "busted" after an initial boom period, others with a mining background are still going strong. Parker, downriver from the Parker Dam, has been important as a trading center for the surrounding mining area. It is also a center for the rich agricultural area nearby, and today it is part of a fast-growing sports community for those who enjoy the pleasures of the Colorado.

Yuma, a thriving Colorado River town of more than 30,000 in the southwestern corner of Yuma County, began as an offshoot of the California gold rush of 1849. When gold was discovered in California and the giant move of people from the East to the West got under way, it was certain that a route for them would be found through southern Arizona. The United States negotiated with Mexico to help trace such a route, and in this first boundary survey in 1849, Lieutenant Amiel Whipple made camp on the California side of the river across from where Yuma is now.

When the gold seekers reached the east bank of the Colorado, they had to cross the river by ferry, and a rather substantial fee was charged for this transportation. Charles Poston and his friends, en route to California in 1854, were unable to pay the fee, so they remained on the east bank and laid out the town of Colorado City.

Many people did not bother going across to California but stayed in Colorado City with the knowledge that gold could be found in the general vicinity.

During the Civil War the post office on the Arizona side of the river was closed, and when it reopened, post-office rules necessitated finding a new name. The one selected was Yuma, the name of the fort directly across the Colorado River, on the California side. Yuma has long been the most important community in the southwestern part of Arizona. Its importance was increased in 1876 when Arizona's first territorial prison was established there. The old prison is now a state historical park. Once a relatively small community handling the merchandise shipped up the river by boats, Yuma is now a major distribution point for the abundance of citrus fruits, cantaloupes, cotton, and other crops grown on the farmlands irrigated by the Colorado. Incidentally, Yuma and the stretch of land downriver from it have the lowest altitude in the state, Yuma being 115 feet above sea level.

The whole saga of the gold seekers coming into Arizona has a personal relevance for me. Yuma County is literally the home county of my family, because my grandfather Michael Goldwater, known to the Mexicans as Miguel Grande, or "Big Mike," was among those who came here looking for gold. Not finding it, he decided to stay, finding his gold instead in the selling of merchandise to others who were searching for the metal.

POPPIES ON SLOPE OF MOUNT AJO

Gold is not the only precious metal that has been sought and found in the Desert Country. Ajo, in western Pima County north of Organ Pipe Cactus National Monument, is a mining town with one of the largest open-pit copper mines in the United States. The smelter to handle the ore once it has been taken out of the open-pit is also located here. Copper, by the way, turned out to be more "precious" than gold in the economic development of the state, for today Arizona produces about 10 percent of the world's total supply of the red metal. The town was once called *Muy Vavi*, which means "warm water" in the Papago tongue. Its present name is the Spanish word for garlic, in commemoration of the wild garlic that grows on nearby hills when weather conditions are favorable.

The mining towns along the bank of the Colorado River—La Paz, Ehrenberg, and Yuma—were important not only as sources of gold, but also as ports for the steamboats that played such an essential role in nineteenth-century commerce. The steamers used to come up the Colorado River from the Gulf of California to Yuma, and eventually they went many miles farther up the river. In the early days the Colorado was a major artery of transportation, bringing people and goods to the river towns and carrying away the precious ore. It was truly the lifeblood of the area.

The Colorado River plays a vital role in the animal life of Arizona as well, and some of the land in the Desert Country has been set aside for the preservation of wildlife. Two of the national wildlife refuges in the Desert Country, the adjoining Cibola and Imperial refuges, protect a stretch of bottomland along the Colorado, and both of them extend into California. The thick growths of mesquite, arrowweed, and salt cedar along the banks provide nesting places for many species of birds, including clapper rails, great blue herons, and white-winged doves. Among the other forms of wildlife are bobcats, raccoons, and mule deer. And occasionally visitors catch a glimpse of horses and burros whose forebears reverted to a wild state after escaping from prospectors.

The Kofa Game Range, located in the center of Yuma County, was established mainly to preserve the habitat of the desert bighorn sheep. Cabeza Prieta National Wildlife Refuge, which stretches along the Mexican border west of Organ Pipe Cactus National Monument, also shelters them, along with the endangered Sonoran pronghorn. This refuge is also the only place in the world where the Kearney sumac can be found.

Though the refuges and the game range were established primarily for the protection of animals and the habitats necessary for their survival, the public is encouraged to make responsible use of them. Anyone wishing to visit Cabeza Prieta must obtain a written permit.

A discussion of the Desert Country would be incomplete without mentioning the Indian reservations that are scattered here and there. The Papago Indian Reservation is the largest one in this part of the state, stretching for some sixty miles along the Mexican border just east of Organ Pipe Cactus National Monument. Because they lived in a remote desert area, the Papago were one of the last tribes to come into contact with the white man, and because of their friendly, sharing nature, they were able

to coexist with white civilization, being the last tribe to be granted a reservation. *Papago* means "Bean People," a reference to their traditional dependence on cultivated beans. Today they depend heavily on raising livestock, and some of them work in the copper mine in Ajo. One of their religious practices involves drinking wine made from saguaro fruit to bring the rain that is essential for growing crops and watering the stock.

The Gila Bend Indian Reservation, a much smaller one some twenty-eight miles to the northwest in Maricopa County, is technically part of the Papago reservation. Both the reservation and the nearby town of Gila Bend got their names from a sharp turn in the Gila River at this point. The section of the Gila River that goes through the Desert Country has little or no water in it most of the time, and Painted Rock Reservoir, which adjoins the reservation, fills with water only after a flood.

In 1970 the land along the Gila in this part of Arizona was designated as a resource conservation area by the Bureau of Land Management. Known as the Fred J. Weiler Green Belt, the conservation area protects a 100-mile stretch of dense thickets that are ideal nesting places for white-winged doves, Gambel quail, and many other birds. The green belt attracts bird watchers and wildlife photographers, as well as hunters.

The other reservations in the Desert Country are on or near the Colorado River. The tribes that live on these reservations have few members today, but they are trying to make a comeback.

The Colorado River Indian Reservation runs along the Colorado in northern Yuma County. (Part of it is across the river in California.) The reservation was established in 1865 for Indians of the Colorado and its tributaries, and at first it was populated by the Mohave and the Chemehuevi, who were long the Mohave's allies. Since 1945, however, Navajo and Hopi Indians have also lived there. The Mohave on this reservation were the first tribe to receive regular rations of beef from the federal government.

Though the Fort Yuma Indian Reservation falls mostly in California, part of it is on the Arizona side of the Colorado. The Indians on this reservation are Quechan. And farther south, in the southwestern corner of the state, are the three sections of the Cocopah reservation. The Cocopah traditionally lived in brush arbors in the summer and in wattled huts in the winter, but now more up-to-date housing is available to them, including mobile homes.

At one time the Indians were the sole inhabitants of the banks of the Colorado. Today this general area is one of the fastest-growing sections of the state. There is hardly a mile or even half a mile along either bank of the Colorado from Davis Dam to Yuma that is not occupied by homes, and the river, with its delightfully blue water and its dams and lakes, has become one of the most popular fishing and water recreation spots to be found in the West. The land along the river that is available for purchase is among the highest-valued real estate in Arizona. When I fly over the once lonesome stretch of water at night, I can see lights along it literally from the Mexican border to the city of Las Vegas. The Desert Country has come a long way.

103

Below– SUNSET-REFLECTING CANAL NEAR YUMA
Right– SAGUARO AND SUN, SONORAN DESERT

The OLD WEST

THE SOUTHEASTERN CORNER OF ARIZONA HAS BEEN THE SCENE OF COUNTLESS REAL-LIFE DRAMAS THAT EPITOMIZE THE SPIRIT OF THE FRONTIER AS IMMORTALIZED IN STORIES, MOVIES, AND TELEVISION PROGRAMS ABOUT THE American West—hence I'm calling this part of the state the Old West. The dramatic action in the region was concentrated in and around two cities, Tombstone and Tucson. At one time the larger of the two, Tombstone has long since seen the glory of its heyday fade. Though it still sustains a small community of some 1,250 people, and has won itself the epithet "The Town Too Tough to Die," Tombstone now serves mainly as a living museum of Arizona's frontier life; in 1962 the U.S. Department of the Interior designated it as a national historic landmark. Tucson's history, on the other hand, is one of persistent upswing. While Tucson participated in the same extravagances of the wild West, and went through a growth period because of its proximity to Tombstone, it did not follow Tombstone's "boom and near-bust" pattern. Tucson has much older roots than Tombstone, going back to the Spanish and even to the Indian past of the Southwest, and instead of diminishing with the retreating frontier, it has continued to grow and diversify.

Tombstone owed its founding in 1879 and its rapid development to prospector Ed Schieffelin's discovery of a rich lode of silver nearby. Schieffelin had been warned by a friend that instead of a mine, he would find a tombstone—meaning that he was likely to be killed by the hostile Apache in the vicinity—and when he found the silver deposit, he named the place Tombstone as an ironic tribute to his friend's concern. When other deposits were discovered nearby, Tombstone became one of the greatest silver camps in the West, and it probably would still be a booming town except for the fact that the tunnels and shafts of the mines kept flooding, and there was no way for the pumps to keep ahead of the water.

In addition to the men who came to work the mines, other people flocked in to get their hands on the miners' gains. Professional gamblers left other cities to descend upon Tombstone, and a large red-light district emerged along with the saloons and dance halls. As though these personal vices were not enough of a problem, there was a prevailing atmosphere of violence, with warlike Apache, cattle rustlers, and the famous Earp-Clanton feud—which culminated in a bloody gunfight at the O. K. Corral in 1881—all contributing to the general disorder. The lawlessness eventually prompted President Chester A. Arthur to threaten Tombstone with martial law.

Actually, Tombstone was no worse than other frontier towns of the period, but it was bigger and so attracted more attention—and more riffraff. Nevertheless, people often overlook the fact that in those days it was also one of the most cultured cities in the West. In the 1880s Tombstone was the largest city between San Francisco and San Antonio, with a population estimated at between 10,000 and 15,000 people. Some of the country's finest entertainers could be seen and heard in the Bird Cage Theatre, and those who desired music on a grand scale could attend the local opera house.

Today the enterprising citizens of Tombstone make sure that the streets and the rest of the old town are maintained pretty much as they were during its heyday. There is an annual three-day celebration in October, appropriately called Helldorado, during which reenactments of the most striking events of the 1880s, including the O. K. Corral shoot-out, are staged. While Helldorado actively recalls the spirit of the past, that same spirit is captured in a quieter form in the original buildings that have been preserved. The Bird Cage Theatre houses a museum, and the Tombstone courthouse—the oldest existing courthouse in Arizona—is now part of a state historic park. An especially silent testimony to the spirit of the past is the Boothill Graveyard, where many of the characters involved in the town's violent episodes were laid to rest. And visitors who come in April can enjoy a breathtaking spectacle of natural beauty in Tombstone. Here, at the Rose Tree Inn Museum, grows what is said to be the largest rosebush in the world, its fragrant white flowers blooming in early April.

In addition to the rich mineral deposits that lured settlers to this area, the broad valley of the San Pedro River, with its fertile soil, was an important reason for the early settlement of southeastern Arizona. The valley, west of Tombstone, was undoubtedly used by prehistoric Indians for north-south travel, and it was later to become one of the major avenues leading north for the early Spanish explorers. The San Pedro is, in fact, the only flowing river in Cochise County. It enters Arizona from Mexico, and at one time it was the second-largest tributary to the Gila River from the south. Some historians maintain that this same river was called *Río Nexpa* by the 1540 Coronado expedition, which is believed to have entered Arizona through the San Pedro Valley. Like the Colorado River, the San Pedro has had many names during the course of recorded history. Colonel James Duncan Graham, for example, referred to it as the *Río Puerco,* or "Dirty River," in 1850.

Coronado National Memorial, a few miles west of the San Pedro River on the United States-Mexico border, commemorates Coronado's opening up of the Southwest to exploration and settlement. Visitors to the memorial can stand atop Coronado Peak and enjoy a magnificent view of the countryside through which the Coronado expedition trekked in its search for the riches of Cíbola. Planned in 1940, 400 years after the brave Spaniards set out across the uncharted terrain, the memorial was established in 1952.

The Chiricahua Mountains, a good forty miles to the east of Tombstone, played an important role in the drama that centered around that city in the 1880s, when it was contributing so much folklore to Western Americana. They were a favorite hideout for the badmen of Tombstone when the forces of law and order were after them. And, as their name implies, they were once the home of the Chiricahua Apache.

Like the other ranges in southeastern Arizona, the steep-sided Chiricahua Mountains punctuate the rolling grasslands with their sudden upthrust. These mountains can be rather easily explored by anyone who enjoys backpacking or horseback riding. I have ridden and walked over most of them, including 9,796-foot-high Chiricahua Peak. Their forested slopes and shady glens, a welcome contrast to the surrounding desert, provide a good habitat for Arizona white-tailed deer.

In the Chiricahua Mountains is Chiricahua National Monument, established in 1924, a wilderness wonderland of unusual geological formations that were eroded into their present—and still changing—shapes by the forces of wind and water. The rock that constitutes these formations was produced millions of years ago by volcanic eruptions. Some of the rock shapes have been given intriguing names, such as Punch and Judy and Big Balanced Rock, a huge mass of hardened lava poised on a pedestal that looks too delicate to bear its weight.

Between the Chiricahuas and the Dos Cabezas Mountains to the north is a twisting canyon called Apache Pass, the scene of many bloody encounters between the Chiricahua Apache and the white man. The trouble started in 1861 when Chief Cochise and a number of his band were lured to the tent of a U.S. Army lieutenant under the guise of friendship and accused of kidnapping and cattle rustling. Though Cochise denied the charges, he was held captive. While he managed to escape, some of the other Apache were hanged, which led Cochise to begin a campaign of revenge against the white man in southeastern Arizona.

Westering emigrants traveling through Apache Pass were sitting ducks for the hostile Chiricahua. The old Butterfield Overland Stage established a station there in 1858, because of the availability of water, and from 1861 to 1874 stage drivers were guaranteed triple pay if they made it through the pass. Many of them did not survive to collect the bonus.

In 1862 several hundred Apache, led by Cochise and Mangas Coloradas, ambushed fifteen Union companies in the pass. The troops were on their way from California to the Rio Grande, hoping to check the Confederates' progress toward the California goldfields. After a fierce battle—the largest ever to take place between Indians and whites in Arizona—the Union soldiers managed to rout the Apache.

The heavy bloodshed soon led to the establishment of Fort Bowie at the eastern entrance to Apache Pass. The fort was built by the Fifth California Volunteer Infantry, and it was named for the infantry's commander, Colonel George Washington Bowie. In 1866 the volunteers were replaced by regular army troops, and two years after that the construction of a new complex of buildings was begun southeast of the original fort. As the problems with the Apache subsided, the fort became less and less important, and it was abandoned as a military post in 1894. Fort Bowie is now recognized as a national historic site. Some of its original walls are still standing, and the Park Service is trying to protect them from the further ravages of time by capping them with adobe.

West of the Chiricahuas and closer to Tombstone are the Dragoon Mountains, probably named after the Third U.S. Cavalry, known as the Dragoons, which was once stationed nearby. The name Dragoon came from the fact that these troops used carbines—called dragoons—instead of the saber and pistol that were usually carried by cavalrymen.

On the east side of these mountains is located an old Chiricahua Apache stronghold now referred to as Cochise Stronghold Memorial Park. It can be reached by following a well-kept dirt road up the side of the mountain, passing from level farming country into a rugged, rockstrewn canyon. The stronghold itself is a large canyon that is open at only one end. The narrow passageway leading into it is guarded by two huge granite boulders, and there is just barely enough space for a car to pass through. The interior of the canyon opens up into a forest glade surrounded by stately oak trees.

Chief Cochise led many raids from the canyon, and for almost twelve years U.S. troops tried in vain to drive him out. Finally, in 1872, one-armed Civil War veteran General Oliver Otis Howard was dispatched to Arizona to seek peace with him. The courageous Howard entered the Apache stronghold unarmed and accompanied only by his aide and by the Apache chief's white blood brother, Tom Jeffords. The general persuaded Cochise and his tribesmen to settle on a reservation encompassing the southeastern Arizona mountains, where they had once ranged freely, acceding to the chief's demand that Jeffords be named the Indian agent.

Cochise died two years after the Chiricahua reservation was established. According to one Apache legend,

he was buried in the stronghold, in a secret cave that was then covered by a landslide, thus concealing his final resting-place from the white man. Another legend holds that his followers galloped their horses up and down the canyon to destroy any trace of his grave.

Peace between the white man and the Chiricahua Apache did not last long, however. In 1876 the Indians were moved from their homeland to the already overcrowded San Carlos reservation farther north, and southeastern Arizona once again became part of the public domain. Many of the Chiricahua, angered by the loss of their territory and by conditions at San Carlos, periodically escaped from the reservation to terrorize the countryside. Other Apache, some led by Geronimo, fled to Mexico.

At one time, some 50 percent of the U.S. Army, stationed at about twenty forts, was in Arizona to fight the Indians. A second post in the vicinity of Tombstone that played an important part in the army's warfare against the Apache was Fort Huachuca, apparently named for a nearby Pima Indian village. Established in 1877 as Camp Huachuca, the post was built at the mouth of Central Canyon in the Huachuca Mountains, some twenty miles southwest of Tombstone. The camp became a permanent post in 1882. After the surrender and exile of Geronimo and his Apache in 1886, which virtually ended the Indian wars in Arizona, Fort Huachuca became relatively quiet. Then in 1910, when the Madero revolution broke out in Mexico, it was made the staging area for the army along the border. The fort remained fairly active for the next thirty years, and during World War II some 22,000 soldiers were stationed there, supplemented by more than 9,000 civilians. At the end of the war, the installation was turned

113

over to the Arizona National Guard, then gradually fell into disuse until the early 1950s, when the army moved the Signal Corps' Electronics Command there.

Today Fort Huachuca is not only one of the oldest of Arizona's army posts, but one of the biggest and certainly one of the most attractive. A visit to the old fort, which is included in *The National Register of Historic Places*, along with Fort Bowie and Tombstone, will show what American military bases looked like before they became the modern establishments they are today. When I took my oath of office as a second lieutenant with the Twenty-fifth Infantry at that fort in 1930, such famous frontier units as the Apache Scouts, used to combat the Chiricahua Apache, were still on duty. Naturally, Fort Huachuca has always held a special interest for me.

Another place in this part of Arizona that has personal relevance for me is the town of Bisbee, located in the Mule Mountains twenty miles south of Tombstone. The history of Bisbee, like that of Tombstone, reaches back into the days of the Old West, and one of the most dramatic episodes of the frontier era had its roots in a Bisbee store owned by my grandfather and great-uncle. It was in the store of Goldwater-Castenada that the famous Bisbee Massacre occurred in 1883. A gang of armed robbers burst into the store and fired into the crowd of shoppers there, killing four of them. The five culprits were tracked down by a hurriedly gathered posse, one of whose members, a saloon keeper named John Heath, betrayed his identity as the mastermind behind the crime when he repeatedly tried to throw off the rest of the posse from the murderers' trail. All six men were brought to trial in the Tombstone courthouse. The five who had actually taken part in the crime were hanged, while Heath was sentenced to a twenty-year jail term. Heath's sentence seemed far too lenient to the angry townspeople, and they took it upon themselves to correct this miscarriage of justice. They borrowed a rope from my family's store and proceeded to Tombstone, where they broke into the jail, seized Heath, and hanged him from a telegraph pole. He was buried in Boothill Graveyard along with the other five desperadoes, and his epitaph reads: "John Heath, taken from County Jail and Lynched by Bisbee Mob in Tombstone, Feb. 22nd, 1884." The coroner's jury absolved the "Bisbee Mob" of any wrongdoing, accepting a coroner's report that Heath had died of "emphysema . . . which might have been caused by strangulation, self-inflicted or otherwise."

One of the biggest attractions in Bisbee today is Brewery Gulch, once known for its drinking sprees and its red-light district. When Bisbee was at its height as a mining town, this was about as wild a place as could be encountered anywhere in the West. The *Brewery Gulch Gazette,* which was first published in 1931, preserves some of the Old West tone that once prevailed here. Another attraction is the Mining and Historical Museum and Civic Center housed in what was formerly the Copper Queen Hotel, where visitors can see a wonderful collection of native minerals, old mining artifacts, and dioramas that demonstrate early mining techniques.

As was true of many Arizona towns, Bisbee came about because of the discovery of copper. In 1877 rich ore samples were discovered in Mule Gulch, resulting in the establishment of the Copper Queen Mine. Other copper deposits were found in the same general area, and by the turn of the century Bisbee was a major boomtown, attracting prospectors and investors from many parts of the world. And today, while the copper has pretty much disappeared, Bisbee continues to thrive as a tourist and retirement town, with a population of about 8,500. An interesting sidelight is that the post office does not provide Bisbee's residents with home delivery, since walking up and down the steep streets would place too great a strain on the mail carriers.

While Tombstone mushroomed into prominence because of its silver and then dwindled to a living museum of its former self, and Bisbee, though able to support a larger population, has lost much of the spirit of its heyday, Tucson has followed a different growth pattern. The oldest city in this part of the state, Tucson has developed more slowly and steadily, and over a considerably longer period of time.

Most of the state's population is concentrated in two places, Phoenix and Tucson. Tucson, whose population of almost 310,000 makes it Arizona's second-largest city, is more of a residential community than Phoenix. It is also much older, going back to the days of the eighteenth-century Spanish missionaries and settlers. And before the coming of the Spanish, the Santa Cruz Valley that cradles the city was the home of many generations of Indians.

Tucson comes from the name of an Indian village, Chuk Shon, that once occupied the same site. The Pima words mean "village at the foot of a black hill"—probably a reference to Sentinel Peak, on the west bank of the Santa Cruz River.

The Spanish history of what was to become Tucson began in 1697, when the Jesuit missionary Eusebio Kino, who was later (1700) to found Mission San Xavier del Bac, passed through the area and commented upon the density of its Indian population. When the Franciscans replaced the Jesuits in New Spain, Father Francisco Garcés took charge of San Xavier. He had a small walled pueblo built near Chuk Shon to protect the Indians there from Apache raids. This pueblo, constructed in 1769, was undoubtedly the origin of the city's nickname, "The Old Pueblo." In 1776 Juan Bautista de Anza established Tucson as a military outpost of New Spain, and his act marked its founding as a permanent settlement.

Tucson remained a small military community for many years, first under Spanish and then under Mexican rule. In 1854 the Gadsden Purchase brought the settlement under the American flag, and it began to grow as a rough-and-tumble town of the Western frontier. Several factors contributed to Tucson's development during the frontier period. Stage lines were routed through the town, where the rough accommodations gave rise to the expression "Tucson bed," meaning lying on one's stomach covered only by one's back. Tucson was chosen as an army distributing point for forts erected against the Apache, and following its incorporation in 1864, it served as Arizona's territorial capital (from 1867 to 1877). The vitality of nearby Tombstone also helped to stimulate Tucson's economy. And like its rowdy neighbor, Tucson went through a wild West phase—"a paradise of devils," traveler J. Ross Browne called the frontier-day town. Crime was rampant, and the judicial system was inadequate to deal with it. One of the most colorful characters of the period was Pete Kitchen, noted for his profanity, his boisterous drinking, and his prowess in fighting the Indians. Today there is a Pete Kitchen Museum near Nogales.

The passing of the frontier period has not abated the city's growth. On the contrary, its population increased fivefold—from 45,454 to 234,600—between 1950 and 1965 alone, and it has achieved importance as a recreational and health resort. Present-day Tucson is known for its attention to the fine arts, and it has probably influenced the cultural life of Arizona more than any other city in the state. The exhibits at the Tucson Museum of Art range from Indian and Spanish-Colonial artifacts to contemporary paintings. In addition to its many displays dramatizing the progression of events leading to Arizona statehood and beyond, the Arizona Historical Society has a unique collection of Western Americana. The Tucson Symphony Orchestra gives a series of concerts every year in the Community Center Music Hall, and the University of Arizona, founded in 1885, offers a whole world of culture that the rest of the city can participate in. The university, which has some 26,600 students, is one of the outstanding institutions of learning in the West. It was here that the famed Dr. Andrew E. Douglass established the principles of dendrochronology, the science of dating very old objects and events by a comparative study of tree rings. Applied to logs and beams found in early Indian ruins, this method has given archaeologists a more precise idea of how old the ruins are. The University of Arizona has several museums of its own and is the site of Steward Observatory, operated in conjunction with Kitt Peak National Observatory, southwest of the city. The facilities at Kitt Peak include the largest solar telescope in the world.

In Tucson Mountain Park, twelve miles west of the city, is a replica of the town as it was in the 1860s, complete with stagecoach rides and pretend gunfights. Old Tucson, as this is called, is both an amusement park and a set for filming movies and television shows about the Old West. Also in Tucson Mountain Park is the Arizona-Sonora Desert Museum, a treasure-house of native plant and animal life. The animals live in facsimiles of their natural habitats. This is a good place for a closeup view of the elusive roadrunner, the bird that is so frequently associated with Arizona in popular art forms.

Every February Tucson is the scene of the Fiesta de los Vaqueros, or the Tucson Rodeo, which opens with a colorful parade of historic vehicles. April is the time of the Tucson Festival, which celebrates the city's cultural heritage with a whole series of events—Indian rituals, a Mexican fiesta, and craft shows.

The terrain surrounding Tucson is remarkable for its natural beauty. Just north of the city are the Santa Catalina Mountains, named by Father Kino. These mountains, with their generous growth of pine trees, are among the loveliest in the entire United States. Their cool, wooded slopes are a mecca for skiers in the wintertime and hikers during the spring and summer. Small streams dart down the mountains, and there are even some lakes. The highest peak in the Santa Catalinas is 9,157-foot-high Mount Lemmon, named for a California botanist who came here with his bride in 1882 to study the flora on its slopes.

Running south off the Santa Catalina Mountains is Rillito Creek, which eventually joins the Santa Cruz River. Beautiful Sabino Canyon was cut into the mountains by the creek's relentless coursing through their midst. This canyon can be explored either on foot or on horseback.

East of Tucson are the Rincon and the Tanque Verde mountains, and to the west are the Tucson Mountains. Considerable stretches of all three ranges fall within the boundaries of Saguaro National Monument, the two units of which flank the city. This national monument is dedicated to the protection of the stately giant of the cactus world, the saguaro, which—except for a few specimens along the Colorado in California—grows mainly in Arizona and northern Mexico. The colossal plant, which weighs several tons at maturity and can attain a height of fifty feet, sometimes lives for as long as two centuries. The yellow-centered white blossom, which blooms in garlands atop its upstretched arms in May and June, is Arizona's State flower.

In addition to the beauty of its flower, the saguaro is a source of food and refuge for some of the animal denizens of the desert. The yet-unfallen fruits and seeds are eaten by birds, and the fallen fruit is food for coyotes, peccaries, and mule deer. Gila woodpeckers and gilded flickers make nest holes in the stems of the saguaro, and after their young have flown away, the holes are taken over by other species of birds. Though Saguaro National Monument was set aside in 1933 primarily to preserve its growths of saguaro cacti, the wide range in elevation of its terrain makes possible a corresponding range in the types of plant life. While saguaro thrive in the low-lying desert areas, the mountain slopes support the growth of ponderosa pines, Douglas firs, and white firs.

Probably the most popular place to visit in the Tucson area is Mission San Xavier del Bac, south of the city. Known as "The White Dove of the Desert," the mission was originally constructed in 1700 by the Jesuits, but it was destroyed half a century later during an Indian uprising and then was rebuilt by the Franciscans. San Xavier del Bac is considered to be the finest example of mission architecture in the United States. Its architectural style embodies several influences—Byzantine, Moorish, Spanish, and Aztec. At the present time much exploratory work is going on to determine the exact locations of the original boundaries of the church, and someday it may be possible to reconstruct the entire mission as it was first built some 280 years ago.

Today the mission stands on the San Xavier Indian Reservation, which is technically part of the Papago reservation. Some 800 Papago live on the San Xavier reservation itself, and over 3,000 more live in nearby Tucson and its environs. The Indians who lived in the Santa Cruz Valley thousands of years ago were probably ancestors of the present-day Papago. Many of the children on this reservation go to a parochial school run by the San Xavier mission, which provides an education for grades one through six, before entering the public school system.

Forty-eight miles south of Tucson, in tiny Santa Cruz County, are the ruins of another old Spanish mission, preserved since 1908 as Tumacacori National Monument. Tumacacori was originally a small Pima village several miles from where the mission now stands. Father Kino said mass there in 1691, and in 1697 the village became a *visita* of the Guévavi Mission to the southeast. (*Visita* is a common term in southern Arizona and northern Sonora. It refers to a place that was too small to afford a mission or church and so was visited occasionally by a padre to keep the interest in religion active.) Following the Pima rebellion of 1751, the village was moved to the present site of Tumacacori, and the Jesuits built a small mission church there. A much larger church, called San José de Tumacacori, was begun at the end of the eighteenth century, after the Franciscans had replaced the Jesuits as missionaries in what is now Arizona. Though it was never completely finished, it was being used by 1822. But the church did not flourish for very long. The Mexican government that replaced the Spanish one converted mission churches to parish churches and expelled the Franciscans, and then Apache raids became a serious problem in the area. Beset by so many difficulties, the Indians of Tumacacori finally abandoned the mission in 1848, and it fell victim to vandals and to the elements. The mission has been restored only to a limited extent since becoming a national monument, but the beautiful displays in the museum there give visitors a good idea of what it might once have looked like.

Just to the north of Tumacacori is the old settlement of Tubac. An earlier Tubac, at a different location, was, like Tumacacori, a visita of Guévavi. The second Tubac started out as a Spanish presidio in 1752, with some fifty military people stationed there, and by 1754 Tubac had 400 or more people. Following the removal of the presidio to Tucson in 1776, Tubac gradually declined to a state of near abandonment, but it revived in 1856 when Charles Poston established the Sonora Mining and Exploring Company there. It was in Tubac that the Territory of Arizona's first newspaper, *The Arizonan*, was published. It was printed on a press brought to Arizona by William Wrightson. He sailed with it around the Horn and then transported it from the west coast of Mexico to Tubac. In the 1860s Tubac again fell into a decline, because of an upsurge of Apache hostilities in the area. Today the ruins of the presidio are protected as part of Tubac Presidio State Historic Park.

The countryside around Tubac and Tumacacori has always reminded me of Spain. In fact, someone who did not know that he was in Santa Cruz County, Arizona, would find it easy to believe without question that this actually was Spain. The climate is always delightful, never too hot, and even though there is some snow in the higher elevations during the winter, it is a comfortable part of Arizona to live in. The county has attracted many people interested in ranching, because it has some of the best cattle country in Arizona. This is what we call mañana country, because of the easygoing, do-it-tomorrow life-style. The guest ranches in Santa Cruz County make it possible for visitors to experience this relaxed way of life.

Although Santa Cruz County nowadays is primarily known for its ranching, the first American settlements were established because of its gold and silver, and mining went on here for many years. At one time it was not uncommon for army officers to invest in mining properties. This gave them an added incentive to try to maintain peace with the neighboring Indians. The Mowry Mine, for example, was named for West Point graduate Sylvester Mowry, who had been assigned to Fort Crittenden. Apprised of the mining potential of Santa Cruz County, he resigned his commission and bought the mine from a group of officers at the fort. Throughout the Patagonia and Santa Rita mountains are many old mining communities, most of them now ghost towns. Ghost towns or not, they are fascinating places to visit.

The largest city in Santa Cruz County is Nogales, a Spanish word meaning "walnuts," and it was so named for the black walnut trees on the site by a surveying crew in the early 1850s. With a population of more than 10,000 people, Nogales is one of the largest cities, and certainly the most prosperous one, on the entire Mexican border. What adds to its attractiveness is the thin line of demarcation that separates it from its sister city, Nogales, Sonora. Only a wire fence running down International Street marks the boundary between the United States and Mexico, and it is the only thing to remind people that there are really two cities instead of one. Nogales plays an important role in the transportation of agricultural goods and livestock to and from Mexico. It has also become a major port of entry for Americans who desire to visit the beautiful country of Mexico. The Mexican city of Nogales, with its many shops and restaurants, is a mecca for Arizonans who seek a brief excursion across the border.

With the entire southern boundary of their state adjoining Mexico, Arizonans share with other Americans and with Mexicans a strong pride in the peaceful, unobtrusive border that has been established between the two nations. Arizonans can also take pride in the harmonious relationships that have been achieved within the boundaries of their own state, where the descendants of the Anasazi Indians and other ancient tribes coexist with the descendants of the early white settlers and with the newcomers seeking business opportunities, fun in the sun, or a place to retire. Having grown up with the state, I have had the opportunity of seeing all of these elements woven into a unified society.

I hope that our armchair journey through this state that means so much to me has been a rewarding one for you. I have tried to describe the magnificence of Arizona's soaring mountains and plunging canyons, the stark beauty of its deserts and plateaus. I have tried to dramatize the spirit of its people, to relate their history and capture the flavor of the places where they live. Since I have had to leave so much unsaid, I am thankful that David Muench's photographs not only illuminate the wonders I have touched upon, but also bring out the many facets of Arizona that eluded the reach of my pen.

Left– McMATH SOLAR OBSERVATORY, KITT PEAK
Above– SAGUAROS AGAINST A FIERY SUNSET
and Below– SAGUARO GROVE IN SAGUARO NATIONAL MONUMENT
Overleaf– SAN XAVIER DEL BAC MISSION

119

Below– BABOQUIVARI MOUNTAINS
Right, top– TOMBSTONE COURTHOUSE
Right, bottom– EYES OF A GHOST—ADOBE RUINS, PEARCE

MODERN HOPI POLYCHROME